PRAISE FOR YOUR AUTHENTIC AWAKENING

"Kara Goodwin's book takes readers on an inner journey to the soul. Simple yet effective techniques are sprinkled throughout the book, enhancing readers' experiences for easier integration and practical application. This book offers a beautiful and natural 'formula' for self-realization, 'aha' moments, and heartfelt energy. Thank you, Kara Goodwin, for your passion, dedication, and loving service to humanity!"

Viviane Chauvet, International Speaker & Founder of the Arcturian University

"In this exploration of Kara Goodwin's insights into the nature of the soul, the reader will discover very plausible ways for connecting to their true self. In sharing her authentic experiences, we can feel the force of creation flowing from her soul into ours, gently urging us out of our own comfort zones into an understanding of reality that stretches us from the known into the unknown. This book offers the power to feel ourselves, the courage to listen to ourselves, the will to know ourselves, and the irrefutable love to be ourselves. There is no better formula for the gift of incarnation than what is laid out here for awakening to our authentic self. Thank you, Kara. Your last name sums up the validation for the practices found here to evolve our spiritual potential as a *good win.*"

Alan Steinfeld, Host, Director, and Producer of *New Realties* TV

"Kara has exquisitely merged her own personal journey of soul-discovery with metaphysical knowledge and spiritual wisdom. She inspires and empowers the seeker to dedicate themselves to the spiritual path. Her guidebook is both an instructional manual for daily spiritual living and a resource for understanding our spiritual design."

Suzanne Ross, Author of the *Up!* book series, Event Producer of Sedona Ascension Retreats

"Kara Goodwin's book provides a personal and heartfelt call to all of us to wake up to who we truly are -- magnificent multi-dimensional spiritual beings incarnated in human form. By providing anecdotes from her own life (which always makes a book fun to read!), Goodwin shares her own experience of awakening and provides tips and exercises for the reader as they engage on their own. A great book for today's spiritual explorer."

Amy L. Lansky, PhD, Author of *Impossible Cure* and *Active Consciousness*

"One of Kara Goodwin's responsibilities in this life is to light the path for others in their quest for spiritual growth and expansion. In *Your Authentic Awakening*, Goodwin digs deep to provide all of us with a cogent and informed road map for living an enlightened life and functioning at a higher frequency. No matter if you are taking your first steps or are an advanced practitioner, this book will gently and intelligently guide you to a more evolved version of you."

Philip Smith, Acclaimed Artist and Author of *Walking Through Walls*

"This book is a breath of fresh air for the modern seeker. Kara Goodwin masterfully guides readers on a journey of self-discovery and conscious living that is both inspiring and practical, offering a balance of deep spiritual insight and real-world application. It reminds us that true awakening is not a distant goal but an ongoing process of remembering who we truly are."

Diana MaAra Divine, Founder of the Source Language Institute

YOUR AUTHENTIC AWAKENING

A Guide to Every Day Spiritual Living

SACRED DRAGON PUBLISHING

LOS ANGELES, CA

Sacred Dragon Publishing Services LLC™
Los Angeles, California
SacredDragonPublishing.com

ISBN: 979-8-9876749-8-7 Paperback
ISBN: 979-8-9876749-9-4 ebook

Cover Design: Emily Mayhill Shoop
Book Design: Ida Jansson, AmygdalaDesign.net
& Julie Murkette, JulieMurkette.com

The information presented in this work is the author's opinion and does not constitute any health or medical advice. The content of this work is for informational purposes only and is not intended to diagnose, treat, cure, or prevent any condition or disease or is meant as a substitute for consultation with a licensed practitioner.

Neither the author nor the publisher assumes any responsibility for errors, omissions, or contrary interpretations of the subject matter herein. Any perceived slight of any individual or organization is purely unintentional. Brand and product names are trademarks or registered trademarks of their respective owners.

Printed in the United States of America

To John, Hayden, and Layla

Thank you for trekking through life with me.
Your love and support allow me to explore my spiritual path
with an open heart and a curious spirit.
You keep me rooted, balanced, and deeply grateful.
I carry your light every step of the way.

TABLE OF CONTENTS

Author's Note

I have taken care to recount my experiences with honesty and authenticity, sharing from the heart the wisdom I've gained through my challenges and missteps. Some real events have been fictionalized when necessary. I have also taken great care to protect the privacy and identities of everyone mentioned in the experiences I have written about. Each person has given consent to be included in this book, and fictitious names have been used unless permission was given to use a true name.

Throughout this book, I have capitalized certain words, such as Higher Self, Pure Source, Universal Consciousness, and Universe. This was a deliberate choice to emphasize the reverence and sacredness I hold for these aspects of the Divine. By highlighting them in this way, I aim to convey their profound significance.

FOREWORD

It is with great joy and profound respect that I introduce *Your Authentic Awakening*, a remarkable guide to spiritual evolution by Kara Goodwin. I first met Kara when she invited me to her amazing podcast. She is a great listener. Her book reflects the wisdom she has garnered as an interviewer and her personal experiences.

In this book, Kara masterfully combines her deeply personal experiences with universal truths, creating a roadmap for those seeking greater alignment with their Higher Self. Her insights resonate with a timeless wisdom that speaks directly to the heart of every seeker.

In a world overflowing with distractions, it is all too easy to lose touch with the quiet voice of the soul. Kara's work serves as a gentle yet powerful reminder to turn inward and reconnect with the divine essence within. Through her thoughtful exploration of meditation, energy work, and multidimensional awareness, she offers readers the tools to rise above limiting beliefs and embrace their full potential.

One of the greatest gifts of this book is its practical approach to spirituality. Kara not only shares her transformative journey but also empowers readers with actionable techniques to navigate their own path. Whether it is reframing negative self-talk, detaching from external influences, or tuning into the synchronicities of life, *Your Authentic Awakening* provides a rich tapestry of practices for growth and transformation.

This book arrives at a pivotal time, as humanity collectively moves toward a higher vibrational state. Kara's emphasis on the interconnectedness of all life and her encouragement to trust divine alignment are more than teachings—they are calls to action. Her work invites us to live more consciously, more lovingly, and more authentically.

As you immerse yourself in these pages, may you feel inspired to embrace your own awakening with courage and grace. Let this book be a trusted companion on your journey, a beacon guiding you toward greater self-awareness, spiritual sovereignty, and the infinite wisdom of Universal Consciousness.

Kara Goodwin has gifted the world a profound resource for transformation. It is an honor to share her work with you, knowing it will touch your heart, elevate your soul, and empower you to step into your highest truth.

Maureen St. Germain

Author, internationally acclaimed ascension teacher, and founder of Saint Germain Mystery School and Akashic Records International

PREFACE

In this book, I have shared glimpses of my spiritual journey, offering personal reflections that mirror broader themes commonly encountered by seekers on their path of awakening. Although the seekers' path is well-worn by countless travelers, each journey is uniquely shaped by the one trekking it. We are all called to forge our own paths, even as we draw guidance and inspiration from the footprints of those who traversed these hallowed grounds before us. Within these pages, I provide the most meaningful lessons I have learned along the way, together with practical suggestions to help you integrate these insights into your own life.

I have explored many different trails along my own spiritual journey. Growing up quasi-religious, my family attended Episcopal services sporadically in my youth. In my teens and early twenties, I broadened my spiritual lens beyond the confines of organized religion, distancing myself from doctrine and devouring personal accounts of direct experiences with the divine, such as near-death experiences, divine interventions, studies on reincarnation, and more. However, over time, I drifted away from nurturing my spiritual curiosities and adopted a more materialistic worldview that prioritized tangible, verifiable experiences over the intangible.

A profound shift occurred in my life following a particularly tumultuous period. It began with the devastating suicide of my sister-in-law, Michelle, who was also a close friend. Her struggle with depression and her untimely passing left a deep wound on my heart.

Soon after, our beloved dog passed away, and my stepdad underwent a delicate spinal surgery. While my stepdad was recovering from the operation, my mother-in-law was hit by a motorbike when crossing the street. Within a month or so of that accident, my stepmom, who had been living with a heart condition for several years, faced rapid decline and ended up in the ICU. Her only hope was a heart transplant, which she miraculously received the day after Thanksgiving.

All of these events unfolded in rapid succession over about a six-month period while my husband and I were living abroad in Italy with our young children, ages 9 and 6. The added stress of trying to balance the responsibilities of our everyday life in Italy with the demands of the family emergencies occurring in America and England quickly became an overwhelming trial. It didn't take long to get to the point where I got a sinking feeling every time the phone rang. Bad news tends to warrant a phone call over a text message.

In processing the stress and grief, a subtle stirring arose within me. I began to feel that there must be more to life than the chaos and fear that I was becoming accustomed to as my life's modus operandi. At the time, I felt disconnected from my soul and wasn't one to pray, but I reached out to God in quiet desperation.

One morning, as I walked home from dropping my kids at school, I directed some thoughts toward God and asked for help. Inwardly, I expressed my longing for clarity and guidance, particularly regarding meditation. Meditation had always intrigued me, but my attempts felt incomplete, as though I was missing an essential element to make it meaningful and productive. With my life in turmoil, I felt a profound pull toward meditation as a potential anchor, and I asked God to lead me to the best starting point if it was truly meant to assist me.

Shortly after that silent request, a series of synchronicities led me to a documentary called *Awake: The Life of Yogananda*.[1] The film, which chronicles the life and teachings of Paramhansa Yogananda, deeply moved me. Yogananda's practical and scientific approach to meditation resonated with my analytical brain, bridging the gap between my practical and materialistic worldview and meditation's esoteric nature. Further synchronicities led me to take courses teaching Yogananda's meditation techniques. Through meditation, I found a renewed peace and calm amidst life's chaos, which led to me becoming certified to teach Yogananda's methods to others.

As I went deeper into meditation explorations, I began to experience myself beyond the limitations of my physical body and thoughts. I gained a profound understanding and acceptance of the energetic nature of physical reality and how it influenced my health and well-being. It was the stepping stone to releasing the grip of my overly analytical perspective and opening up to the mystical, intuitive aspects of reality that fostered trust in insights and wisdom that transcended my traditional senses. I became insatiably curious about spiritual truths and concepts such as energy healing, psychic phenomena, and prayer.

That thirst for understanding the world from a spiritual perspective inspired the creation of *The Meditation Conversation* podcast. The podcast began in 2018 as a collaborative project with Alessandra Kylin, a fellow student of Yogananda's methods. Eventually, I became the sole host and recast the platform in 2025 as the *Soul Elevation* podcast to encompass a broader range of topics focused on expanding consciousness. The podcast platform has brought me the profound joy of interviewing hundreds of guests on a wide range of esoteric topics, from quantum entanglement to communicating with the dead to miraculous healings.

The knowledge I have gained through my own spiritual experiences and learning inspired me to support others in strengthening their connection to their souls and Higher Selves through meditation, Reiki, retreats, and spiritual counseling. With this book, I bring that same support and encouragement to a broader audience, offering insights, concepts, and truths to enrich your spiritual journey.

My understanding and the words and concepts I refer to throughout this book have been shaped by the lineages and teachings that have grabbed my attention over the years and helped me to put language to experience. These teachings include the work of Paramhansa Yogananda, my mentor

Michael Massey, courses and books by spiritual teachers such as Ram Dass, Maureen St. Germain, Neale Donald Walsch, Sandra Walter, and many, many others I've engaged with over the years.

With that broad spectrum of wisdom teachings in my spiritual lexicon, some of the terms used in this book may be new to you; others may be familiar but used in ways that differ from your understanding. While I've clarified contextual meanings where needed, I encourage you to focus on the essence of the concepts discussed rather than get hung up on the technicalities of word choice. Debating semantics can distract from recognizing core truths that may be expressed differently by teachers and lineages.

The insights I share here are based solely on my personal perspective. Each spiritual journey is unique, and my hope is that you will carry with you what is valuable to you on your path. May you find ample nourishment for your soul within the pages ahead.

INTRODUCTION

This book was written with the curious in mind. If you are drawn to this content, you are ready to journey into the mystical. I've written it from my heart in a way that is authentic to my true nature, and it will most deeply resonate with those interested in exploring the treasures hiding beneath the surface of the typical life experience.

We are embarking on a journey together. While the distance to be traveled is unimaginably close, its path is more challenging than climbing the highest peak, swimming the widest sea, or exploring the deepest cave. Yet, the rewards that await are beyond measure.

At the core of our expedition lies the concept of spiritual design. While we are all familiar with the physical aspects of life - the body, emotions, and thoughts – there is a profound element that often goes unacknowledged, particularly in Western cultures: the soul.

As we set our sights on this life-changing destination, let's ensure we are heading in the right direction by checking our metaphorical compasses and aligning our understanding of common terms. Metaphysical terminology varies between lineages and teachers, so let's take a moment to clarify potentially ambiguous terms you'll encounter on our journey.

UNDERSTANDING SPIRITUAL DESIGN CONCEPTS

To grasp the essence of the spiritual design, it is essential to have some familiarity with fundamental terms and concepts that will frequently arise on your journey of soul awakening. Let's shine a light on these terms to eliminate misunderstandings and make the most of our odyssey.

Source

A grand universal intelligence runs through everything. I call this intelligence Pure Source Consciousness, or Source. To me, this is the same as God or Universal Consciousness. Everything comes from Source, and ultimately, everything and everyone returns to Source.

Higher Self

The Higher Self refers to the extension of you that exists beyond the human form. Our human bodies are temporary expressions of the Higher Self, an eternal expression of Source. The Higher Self is infinite and timeless. It has experienced many different human incarnations, perhaps even lifetimes on other planets or other dimensions of reality.

I relate to the Higher Self as a stream of sentient and intelligent high-frequency energy or light. While most of the Higher Self exists in a higher realm that is invisible to us as humans, a fractal, or part, of our Higher Self energy takes form in our body and expresses itself as the soul through our human experience. In human form, we can strengthen our connection to this higher consciousness stream of light, which is the Higher Self, expanding the body's Divine light and energy. We can, alternatively, disassociate from our Higher Self, limiting our human experience to only that which can be perceived through our five senses— sight, sound, touch, taste, and smell.

While our Higher Self is unseen, our human aspect has a physical form and individuated identity as a body and personality. The human form has a beginning and an end— birth and death. Different schools of thought use various words to describe our embodied human aspect, such as ego, small self, little self, or simply self with a small *s*. I affectionately refer to my human form self as little Kara in contrast to my Higher Self.

The way we humans experience life makes it natural for us to relate to the Higher Self as a kind of etheric person located above us. However, I see the Higher Self as a massive, expansive stream of energy that has condensed into a container of flesh, thought, emotion, and activity, which we experience as being human. Our Higher Self exists in higher levels of consciousness in a timeless state. Conversely, our human expression experiences linear time, with a history it remembers, a future it can imagine, and a present moment happening now.

Soul

The soul exists within the human form as a fragment of our Higher Self. Just as our Higher Self is a fractal of Source, so is the soul a fractal of our Higher Self. The Higher Self takes part of itself to create a soul to experience individuality. It repeats this process many times to form many souls, each with a unique journey. This cycle of creation is experienced as reincarnation. Our Higher Self is portioning itself into various beings to experience different life scenarios, both here on Earth and across other planets and dimensions.

The soul is the invisible animator of the body. You are not a body that has a soul. Rather, you are a soul temporarily contained in an incarnated human body. When the body ceases to function, the soul exits the body and rejoins the Higher Self in higher realms of existence. The soul uses the body as a vehicle to navigate the physical realm and express itself on the Earth plane.

An easy analogy to illustrate the Source-Higher Self-soul-human relationship is the ocean. In this analogy, Source is like the ocean. Fill a cup from the ocean, and you have the Higher Self. The water in the cup is comprised of many drops. Each drop of the water in the cup is an individuated soul expression of the Higher Self. Take a drop of water out of the cup, and you have the human form. In the same way that a drop taken out of the cup is separated from its original Source—the ocean, humans experience a sense of separation from their original Source—Pure Source Consciousness.

Consciousness

Source, Higher Self, human self, animals, trees, plants, and all sentient life have consciousness. We are all united through different levels of collective consciousness, from our local collective all the way to the unified field of Pure Source Consciousness. Yet, we each are a unique individuated expression within these greater fields of unified consciousness. Our spiritual journey of connecting with our Higher Self involves progressively expanding our awareness and connecting with higher levels of consciousness.

One level of our shared consciousness is the human collective consciousness that we influence and are influenced by as a part of our human experience. I think of this collective consciousness as an invisible web of consciousness that connects us and carries the thoughts and energy of every human on the planet. An easy way to understand this is to think of common phrases that have become popular in the collective lexicon. For example, even if you have never seen the Bud Light commercial where the word *whassup* was first used decades ago, it has so thoroughly wormed its way into the collective consciousness that you have likely asked or been asked, "Whassup?"

Our individuated consciousness expands as we mature spiritually. An analogy to understand the concept of expanding consciousness is an imaginary box. The imaginary box represents your current version of reality. What you understand as being real or possible is in the box; anything you perceive as not real or impossible is outside the box. As your consciousness expands, you begin to have realizations and experiences that don't fit in your imaginary box because they don't match the version of reality in your box.

For example, you may suddenly develop an interest in meditation, whereas before, anything to do with meditation didn't fit in your box. But now, you seek out information about meditation and learn how to do it. You integrate meditation into your daily life, and what used to be outside your box is now inside the box, expanding your field of awareness.

Multidimensional Awareness

As you expand your consciousness, you access new levels or layers of consciousness and add new possibilities to your imaginary box, including an awareness of a multidimensional reality. Multidimensionality is similar to the concept of multiple perspectives or multiple data points that can all be true at the same time.

While there are much more comprehensive ways to understand the vast scope and reach of multidimensional realities, a simple approach to this concept is considering that the unseen world exists in the time and space continuum just as much as the seen world. Experiencing multidimensional awareness requires letting go of the belief that only the seen world exists or that we can only experience a physical world. Think of experiencing life through the five senses as just one dimension of experience. Because the physical objects we see have height, width, and depth, we often describe this dimension of existence as the third dimension.

If you are willing to consider levels of existence beyond the third-dimensional realm, here are some examples of how you might experience another dimension through multidimensional awareness: experiencing a past life moment, having contact with the spirit of a loved one who has passed, engaging in astral travel, or interacting with an extraterrestrial life form or consciousness. Having any of these experiences requires accessing a dimensional layer of existence other than the third-dimensional one we are familiar with.

Expanding into higher levels of consciousness requires letting go of the linear, dualistic perception of real and illusion. Using the imagination as a tool allows us to open new pathways within our brains and energy fields, enabling experiences outside our concept of possibility to happen and setting the stage for multidimensional experiences.

As you experience yourself more from the perspective of consciousness beyond your human form, you become aware that there is order and connection throughout all creation. Life doesn't appear to be random. Because you are allowing yourself to perceive in a multidimensional way, you can start to notice patterns. Similarities, or synchronicities, appear to connect different parts of your life.

As your consciousness expands to an awareness of multidimensionality, it is common to notice synchronicities coming into your awareness. I like to think of synchronicities as coincidences with a higher purpose. It's a way we get confirmation from the Universe that we are seen. A synchronicity can manifest as the same message being delivered to you from different sources, repeating numbers, experiences that seem to fall into place with little to no effort on your part, or a chance encounter with someone who is a catalyst for change in your life in big or small ways. It is as though the Universe is organizing itself and everything at its disposal in just the right way to usher in exactly what you need.

Mind

Another aspect of the human experience is the mind. Whereas the Higher Self is connected to Universal Consciousness, our mind perceives its experience from a much more limited perspective relating to its beliefs, preferences, sensory inputs, previous experiences, and other factors explored in Chapter 1.

We often associate the human mind with the brain, but it is not the same thing. Scientific research suggests the mind is nonlocal to the brain. In other words, the mind is not confined to the brain. I use the term mind to denote how we receive and process information. The brain is part of how we take in information, but our bodies also have other receptors that respond to incoming information. In addition to the thoughts we may think at any given time, we also get signals from elsewhere in the body. A stressful thought can cause a response in our gut. A loving thought can cause a warmth or glowing feeling in our heart center. The throat might feel tight when we feel repressed. These are examples of intel we receive directly from our bodies that contribute to the knowing of the mind. The totality of all the ways we receive information makes up the mind, not only the intellectual thoughts in the brain.

Everything is Energy

Everything is energy, including consciousness. So, having some understanding of energy is imperative to expanding consciousness. Fundamental to understanding energy is some familiarity with the concept of frequency and vibration. These terms are often used interchangeably, but there is a difference. Vibration is the oscillation of particles. An example of vibration is the pulsating sensation when a cat purrs. You can also see the vibration in a plucked guitar string or pulsating loudspeaker vibrating with sound.

Everything vibrates at specific rates, and the measurement of that rate of vibration is its frequency. The unit of measurement for frequency is hertz (Hz). Frequencies determine and differentiate vibrational patterns. Energy is carried on the vibration. A higher frequency carries more energy than a lower frequency.

Because energy is nontangible, it can be difficult to understand its validity or that it truly plays a role in physical reality. However, we are familiar with the force of energy in its practical use in the physical world, such as microwaves, radio waves, and Wi-Fi. We use these things every day. They are invisible but have real-world implications of quickly cooking our food, allowing us to hear broadcast music instantaneously, and sending and receiving information on our devices.

Sound and light are also energy. The human body is particularly attuned to sound and light through our sensory abilities to see, hear, and feel the physical world. We can see light and hear sound but also feel their energy. An example of feeling the vibrational frequency of sound is the shock wave we feel in our body from loud booms, such as fireworks or explosions. We can also feel the energy of heat radiating out from the sun.

Energy is not contained to the world of the invisible. Things that appear solid are also energy. Matter is compressed energy, as expressed in Einstein's famous discovery $E = mc^2$, showing that mass and energy are equivalent. You are actually the embodiment of this equation. Your human body may seem solid, but it is energy. Shifting your understanding to solid objects being energy paves the way for understanding how you can be influenced by energy, even though energy is invisible, and your body is not.

Your spiritual design comprises the Higher Self, soul, body, and mind. None of these aspects of you are siloed; they all work together to create the beautiful and complex being that you are. Consciousness flows through each aspect of your spiritual design and connects you to all sentient life. As you expand your consciousness and increase your vibration, you understand life in a multidimensional way and experience synchronicity.

Now that our compasses are aligned and the fundamental concepts of spiritual design have been clarified, let's begin our journey of authentic spiritual awakening!

CHAPTER 1

HEARING THE SOUL

Your soul is talking to you all the time. Perhaps you already hear its familiar voice and warm hello. Even if you haven't heard your soul's hello yet, it's there, lovingly waiting for you to awaken to its subtle impulse. Perhaps you haven't heard your soul talking to you because you think you haven't followed some prescribed formula to initiate its communication. Maybe you believe the obstacle is that you don't meditate, you don't meditate long enough or deeply enough, you haven't been to the right psychic, the stars haven't had the right alignment, or you've never taken ayahuasca to facilitate the meeting of your soul. In fact, none of those things have kept you from hearing your soul.

Typically, we don't hear our souls talking because it's a gentle, quiet voice that gets lost in the noise of modern living as we rush from one thing to the next. All day long, we distract ourselves by scrolling on our phones, attending to a never-ending list of to-dos, and numbing ourselves in clever ways like shopping, alcohol, or binge-watching. Rarely are we giving ourselves the right environment to hear the subtle messages of our soul. Although the soul's voice is naturally quiet, if it's habitually ignored, it will shout its messages in more and more pronounced ways that may eventually present as an illness, accident, loss, or other crisis. Fortunately, when you know how to tune in and receive your soul's guidance, it doesn't need to resort to such drastic measures of hitting you over the head to be heard.

Another reason you may not be hearing your soul talking is that your logical mind tells you to listen for it with your ears. While ears are a neat little way to hear the sound of your daily life, the soul isn't limited to the physical senses. Its whispers can be too fine to be heard with your ears. Its signs can be too sneaky to be caught by your eyes. Its touch can be so close it feels like sensations your body is making inside you.

The soul is clever beyond its creative, communicative capabilities. It connects you to the invisible, spiritual realm where your Higher Self resides and is with you every step of the way in your physical existence. You can make subtle changes in your everyday life to attune yourself to your soul, allowing your spiritual side to flourish. Being able to receive your soul's guidance can alter your life in both small and wondrously magnificent ways. It can shift your perspective about how meaningful your existence is and how truly loved you are. Establishing or deepening your connection with your soul allows you to experience more joy as you open yourself to the spiritual side of life. As your focus shifts to your soul, wealth, possessions, power, and control that drove you in a material-focused world lose their influence and significance in your life. Instead, simple experiences like a shared moment of joy or a small gesture of kindness that had been taken for granted are now received and seen as significant to your soul.

It is safe to say that if these words are finding their way to your eyeballs at this moment, you are, in fact, receiving at least some guidance from your soul, whether it feels like it or not. Every day you are alive, you are creating your life. When you feel that pull toward creating and living your life from the place of the soul, exciting new areas of exploration are opening to your awareness. It's not about turning your life upside down to experience a deep connection with your soul. It's about incorporating new practices and perspectives into your existing life.

CONNECTING WITH YOUR HIGHER SELF

A fundamental step on the path to living from the soul is connecting with your Higher Self. In this chapter, we will explore concepts of spiritual awakening relating to the Higher Self and higher levels of consciousness. These concepts will be the background against which we will build practical applications to foster that awakening in subsequent chapters. Experiencing life from the third-dimensional, material world perspective is different than a perspective that comes from a higher level of consciousness, from where your Higher Self operates. These shifts of viewpoint lay the groundwork for spiritual living.

Despite the unprecedented opportunity we now have to connect with higher consciousness in this time of accelerated awakening and transformation, most people choose to limit their awareness and experience to the physical realm. Like drowsy bears who are slow to emerge from their hibernation den, they are not quite ready for the soul awakening necessary to connect with their Higher Selves. This is an observation without judgment. Each individual is on their own journey of growth and evolution. No one is getting this wrong. Only the soul knows when the time is right to begin expanding awareness into the unknown, the unseen—the spiritual realm.

Even if someone is not interested in developing a connection with their Higher Self right now, the potential for that connection is always there, ready for engagement. Everyone has the ability to connect with their Higher Self and the unbounded potential of that union to bring delight and surprise in brand-new ways.

There is an adage that a cave may remain in darkness for millennia, but the strike of a single match instantly illuminates what had been hidden from view. I find this to be a helpful analogy for understanding how the mind remains shrouded in darkness until the spark of awareness illuminates the truth about the higher levels of consciousness that have been hidden from view.

For me, it has been a long journey from living only in the known physical world to trusting that which cannot be explained in physical, material terms. To be honest, I still don't *always* trust concepts, interpretations offered by others, or perceived intuition that are not easily explained through my understanding of the physical world. It feels important to apply discernment and understand that sometimes fantasy could be mistaken for truth. I often see examples of people making leaps about the meaning of an event or experience that doesn't feel completely true to me. Applying discernment involves not only using my mind to determine if something makes sense to me but also feeling into the subtle sensations within the body. Sensations such as a feeling of expansion, upliftment, or warmth in the heart feel affirmative to me, while a contraction, drop, or sinking feeling seems like my body is telling me no. Throughout this book, you will be given many practical ways to tap into and fine-tune your own abilities to read the cues being given beyond your intellect to assist in your discernment.

Do We Create or Receive Thoughts?

In the introduction, I differentiated between the mind and the brain. I invited you to consider the mind not only as your brain and thoughts but also as communication signals coming from the body, such as the subtle sensations used for discernment mentioned in the previous paragraph. So, let's look at the role of your thoughts in reaching new levels of consciousness.

Thoughts can come to us that seem to have no explicable origin within our brain. Have you ever had someone pop into your head without a known trigger, and then that same person calls you? Did you think about them first, or did their thought of you spark your thoughts of them? Clearly, they were thinking of you right before they called you. You got the signal in your mind before the phone got the signal. So perhaps there was something outside of both of you that sparked simultaneously, putting you each in the other's mind.

One morning, as I was breaking through the surface to wakefulness from the depths of sleep, I thought my husband should consider going to England soon to see his mom, who had not been well. I mentioned it to him a few minutes later.

He said, "It's funny you should say that because I just had the exact same thought."

From my perspective, the thought had come to me out of nowhere. But when my husband told me he had the same idea, it occurred to me that the thought about his mother was floating outside us, and both our minds picked it up.

A similar experience that still makes me laugh involved a seemingly spontaneous text message. I took our son to tennis practice and then ran an errand. My husband was on a call when I left, so I hadn't been able to tell him that I wasn't coming right back as usual. The errand took longer than expected, and after a while, I texted my husband to let him know my whereabouts. He commented on the funny timing of my text because he had just been wondering where I was.

I replied, "I know."

When I got home, my husband asked me how I knew he was wondering where I was right before I texted him.

I couldn't come up with a response other than, "I just knew."

He started guessing rational things about how I could have known, like seeing him on one of the security cameras getting up to look for me.

"No, nothing like that," I told him.

"What, telepathy then?" he finally guessed.

I just laughed and shrugged, thinking it was certainly more along those lines because I hadn't checked the cameras. With that, we both started laughing. My husband is not into the workings of consciousness like I am, but he has a curious mind and a light heart.

Reflecting more on what prompted my text, I realized that it wasn't so much telepathy in that I didn't specifically know that he was wondering where I was at that exact moment. Instead, I had acted on an impulse to let him know where I was that simultaneously matched his wonderings about where I was.

Both of these examples with my husband illustrate each of us tuning in to or receiving the same thought at the same time. If we think of consciousness connecting all things, it could be that rather than both of us organically *developing* the thought at the same time, we *received* it at the same time from the greater consciousness that we are a part of and is much bigger than us.

So, do we create our thoughts or receive them? Perhaps we are doing both in a nuanced dance that human logic is only beginning to understand.

INFLUENCE OF COLLECTIVE CONSCIOUSNESS

In the introduction, I presented the concept of human collective consciousness as an invisible field connecting everything. Our thoughts, feelings, actions, and energy, as well as those of everyone around us, are floating around in the shared space of our local community, state, country, and world, affecting the consciousness of all living things and beings. Even if we are completely oblivious to the field of collective consciousness around us, we still absorb the information and energy emanating from it. As we expand our consciousness, we become less oblivious and more aware of what we pick up from collective consciousness. We discern more easily when we are tuning into something from the collective consciousness that is not originating from within our own consciousness or experience but is causing an emotional response or feeling within us, nonetheless.

I experienced a great example of collective consciousness influencing someone's feelings on January 6, 2021, the day rioters stormed the United States Capitol building. I met up with my mentor, Michael Massey, to run errands for a retreat we were putting together. As soon as I saw Michael, I knew something was wrong. In contrast to his typically friendly and relaxed demeanor, he was anxious and emotional—a golden retriever caught in a sudden thunderstorm. I asked what was bothering him, but he couldn't pinpoint anything specific. He said it was just a feeling that something was really wrong. He pushed past the feeling so we could continue with the errands, but he remained in a state of high alert. While running errands, we talked about what might be disturbing him. An inventory of what was going on in his life didn't yield anything out of the ordinary, and eventually, Michael surmised that what he was feeling wasn't *his*. He was tuning into something that was happening at a collective level.

Later, while we were sitting at my kitchen table, I opened a news app on my phone to see if any breaking news could explain Michael's mysterious feelings. There it was! New blasts about the insurrection riots in Washington, D.C., flooded my news stream. When I shared the news with Michael, he looked at me with wide eyes, revealing his inner confirmation about the cause of his unsettled feelings.

I have also had many experiences of feelings that I couldn't explain and that didn't match what was happening in my life. An example is a sudden sadness that came out of nowhere while walking my dog by a particular spot in my neighborhood. For several days, I felt the same sadness when I walked past this spot. I combed through the happenings in my personal life that may have warranted the unsettled feelings but didn't find a matching set of cause and effect to explain the sadness. Eventually, when I recognized the pattern of repeatedly experiencing this feeling in the same area of the neighborhood, I suspected I was picking up on emotional energy coming from the field of consciousness in that proximity. In short, I was experiencing someone else's sadness.

EXPANDING AWARENESS TO ELEVATE CONSCIOUSNESS

Connecting to higher levels of consciousness requires us to keep expanding our awareness and be open to new possibilities and understandings. If we are fixed and rigid about what we believe is possible, we will never have room within us to allow for new understandings or experiences. For instance, imagine you hear or read an inspiring passage introducing something you thought impossible, like past and future lives. With a rigid and inflexible perspective, you will dismiss the new information because it doesn't fit your current worldview. You will not explore the idea nor discover something new in order to preserve your perception of reality. If, instead, you suspend your current beliefs in order to explore something you'd never considered before, you may learn things you didn't previously know. Through this exploration, you discover very plausible explanations and research that you have never seen before. You open yourself up to all kinds of new information and ways to see the world because you stay in a state of allowing instead of restricting your worldview to reinforce what you already believed. You allow your imaginary box discussed in the introduction to get a bit bigger.

As you continue exploring new concepts, you may experience enhanced sensory perceptions, such as seeing light or colors differently or perceiving a light within you for the first time. You may sense this new experience as something meaningful, inwardly communing with you. You didn't know that it was even possible to see the light inside yourself or feel that there were parts of yourself that could be revealed through expanded awareness. But now, through your openness to expand into new experiences and understanding, your imaginary box gets a bit bigger to fit this new aspect of experience.

As your consciousness continues to expand and open, each new awareness builds upon the other, like each new brick in a foundation building on the others to support the structure. This expansion happens through learning from the wisdom teachings of those you trust who came before. As you become more open and drawn to learning about things that expand consciousness, you will attract information and experiences to help you on your path. You may find certain books, podcasts, or presentations show up in your life to explain concepts or share experiences you didn't think possible. Hearing about the experiences of others gives you a roadmap or understanding to offer context for experiences that aren't talked about in mainstream outlets.

But the most compelling additions to that imaginary box come from direct experience. The most remarkable experiences of expanding consciousness will be your own, purely because those are completely undeniable. You know what you experience, even if you can't easily explain it to others. And if others don't believe you, it is just an indication that they don't yet have a frame of reference to understand; their box doesn't contain the components at this time to be able to fit your experience into reality as they know it. You know what is true because you have seen it for yourself, and your box has room to hold it.

MULTIDIMENSIONAL AWARENESS

As you continue to expand your awareness to connect to Higher Consciousness, your understandings and experiences may start to take you beyond the boundaries of the third-dimensional, material world. How you perceive reality may begin to shift as your awareness becomes multidimensional. You are like a butterfly just emerging from the confines of its cocoon. As it takes its first flight, the experience of its new perspective is unfathomable from its limited ground-level experience as a caterpillar.

Multidimensional experiences can be difficult to comprehend because they exist outside of time and space as we know it. They require us to let go of the physical realm and Newtonian-based laws of physics as the only possible explanation of reality and our existence within it. Many of my personal experiences of multidimensional awareness have involved interacting with geometric symbols and light in a non-physical way that I can see with my eyes open or closed, and often in a 360-degree way. In these inner experiences, light and color seem to organize into shapes and designs in an intelligent way beyond how we typically receive information in our everyday experiences. I share more about this in later chapters.

On the opposite side of the spectrum of multidimensional awareness is linear thinking. Linear thinking is a straight-line perspective with a single view that A caused B. For instance, a linear understanding of how a plant came to exist would be that a seed was planted (A) and then grew into a plant (B), cause and effect—end of story. However, from a multidimensional way of thinking, the perspective expands to consider factors and influences beyond simple physical cause and effect, such as the plant's connection with nature and Earth, the source of inspiration, or the impetus to plant the seed.

From a multidimensional perspective, you might realize that a greater intelligence, which we can call Source, conspired with the person planting the seed to ensure it grew in the most beneficial spot for the plant and Earth. Source could have simply carried the seed on the wind or inspired an animal to eat the plant and deposit its droppings in that exact location. Stretching the multidimensional possibilities even further, Source could have used a being beyond human perception, like a fairy, to place the seed precisely where it was most needed.

Notice that in each potential explanation for how a plant came into physical existence, the effect appears to come prior to the cause, whereas, in the third dimension, we believe the cause precedes the effect. Engaging in multidimensional awareness allows us to hold many potentialities beyond what is commonly accepted in our physical, material world.

IMAGINATION AS A GATEWAY TO EXPANDING CONSCIOUSNESS

Stretching into higher levels of consciousness requires being open to understanding reality in a new way. In order to experience new ways of being, you must be willing to let go of fixed ideas about reality. Your imagination is an ally in exploring new ways of thinking and reaching higher levels of consciousness.

A big challenge for me has been embracing my imagination and letting go of the need to classify experiences as *real* or *imagined*. I am a rational person by nature, so when I started receiving insights or tapping into something beyond my little Kara self, I was quick to try to classify whether I was indeed experiencing and connecting with something bigger than my little Kara self or whether it was wishful thinking. Was it real, or was I imagining it? But being in that framework of judging the *realness* of something is energetically contracting. Dismissing an experience as *not real* closes us off energetically. Labeling an experience as merely coming from the imagination can limit our engagement with higher consciousness, like navigating an expansive city with a rudimentary or outdated map. Cutting off imaginative insights restricts the flow of consciousness that could lead to profound understanding and hinders exploration of the depths and layers of our awareness. Remaining in an open state and resisting the urge to classify between real and imaginary allows curiosity and exploration, enhancing our perception of reality beyond the tangible.

The imagination is also a gateway or portal into more visceral experiences of higher consciousness. We require imagination to usher in new possibilities of understanding. Multidimensional experiences, by their very definition, expand us out of the limitations of the third dimension. Understanding experiences from a multidimensional lens requires the help of the imagination to consider concepts and ideas that push against what is commonly understood to be true in the physical, material world.

Consider, for instance, perceiving a quick flash of light in your peripheral vision. You may have heard it suggested that a sparkle or flash of light in your peripheral vision is one way spirit guides, departed loved ones, or others in the invisible realm communicate with incarnated humans. This experience may make you question whether the vision was something more, perhaps a form of communication. You *know* the experience of seeing the flash of light was real because you saw it. But to move past the physical perception, the imagination must engage and open you to the possibility of the experience as meaningful communication from a loving being in another dimension. Without that spark of possibility created in the imagination, the rational mind cannot expand beyond the physical constructs.

Being open to the possibility that the flash of light was spirit communication is not a big leap if you already know it's a possible way to experience that type of communication. But if you believe that an experience outside of the rules of the material, physical world only belongs to the imagination and, thus, is not real, you may deny yourself the opportunity to have a surprising, meaningful experience with higher consciousness in your everyday life.

SYNCHRONICITY AWARENESS

As you expand your awareness and strengthen your connection to your Higher Self, you will notice the Universe seeming to organize itself to deliver messages, drive points home, inspire, give instruction, or simply remind you that you are seen and loved. These messages can come to you as synchronicities with precise timing that fall into place with little to no effort on your part.

I have lost count of how many times I've discussed an obscure topic with my spiritual mentor, Michael, only to come across the same topic in a book later that same day. Because the obscurely specific topics covered in our conversations are almost immediately reinforced in my reading, it is crystal clear to me that these synchronicities with Michael are Divine orchestrations, drilling home the relevance and truth of the message received.

Another example of synchronicity related to books is when different books I am reading have the same message for me. I have been fascinated by how often different books written years apart by authors from various parts of the world with different spiritual perspectives reinforce the same concept. When exploring a specific metaphysical concept point, I often hear or read the same point repeatedly from multiple sources. It is as though these disparate books and talks are entwined in a beautiful dance that is deliberately weaving through my life to illuminate a new truth in my awareness. I think of these instances as synchronicities on steroids.

Another way I experience synchronicity is when one topic keeps emerging from different sources. A good example of this is an experience I had when praying frequently for a client's wife who had just passed. During lunch with a friend, I was sharing my sadness about this unexpected death when I clearly overheard a woman seated a few tables away say the wife's name. I subtly turned my attention toward the other table, but mysteriously, I couldn't make out a word they were saying once I deliberately tried to hear their conversation. Then, an older German couple who spoke very little English stopped at our table. In our sparse conversation, the woman shared her name, which, amazingly, was again the name of my client's wife. The way this name came up multiple times, particularly when I was sharing about her passing, felt like a higher consciousness was communicating that my heartfelt prayers had been received.

Another way we can experience synchronicity is by noticing repeated patterns or numbers. For instance, some people frequently see repeating 4s in various places. These repeating 4s jump out at them, even when most people would not notice them, illustrating synchronicity in their world. You might find yourself looking at the clock exactly when it's 1:11, 2:22, 3:33, and so forth or noticing specific repeating numbers on license plates, receipts, and phone numbers. These synchronicities can feel like gentle nudges from the Universe to pay attention and consider a deeper meaning connecting all aspects of your life.

If you want to continue to experience life in a mundane, materialistic way, then continue to live and think the way you always have. But if you want to engage with higher consciousness and incorporate a more spiritual perspective to living, then some changes to how you think and understand reality will facilitate that desire. As we have explored, several methods for attuning to your soul work together to align you with receiving guidance from your Higher Self. Establishing and strengthening the connection to the Higher Self requires expanding your consciousness and being willing to hold a multidimensional perspective. Multidimensional awareness embraces the imagination and releases the grip of the linear, rational mind. As you become more attuned to your soul's communication, patterns will begin to reveal in your life as you experience synchronicities.

do it!

You can strengthen your ability to hear your soul and connect to your Higher Self anytime. For best results, especially if you are new to these concepts and the practice of meditation, you want to set aside a few minutes where you will have no distractions. Be alone, seated upright and comfortable, and have no TV or music on.

- Close your eyes.

- Take some deep breaths down low in your tummy.

- Notice your body parts. Notice your legs. You have legs, but your body is more than your legs. Notice your shoulders. You have shoulders, but your body is more than your shoulders. Move through other parts of your body, noticing each part with an awareness that they are part of your body, but your body is much more than its parts.

- Notice noticing your body. The part of you that is noticing your body is not your body. You are noticing your body as an awareness. Your body and your awareness of your body are different but intertwined.

- Be this awareness, feeling yourself breathing, noticing your body, noticing the self that is aware of your body, until you are ready to open your eyes.

CHAPTER 2

OBSTACLES ON THE PATH TO HIGHER SELF CONNECTION

Not every journey is a straight shot from start to finish. Sometimes, we encounter obstacles and detours along the way that cause us to adjust our plans. We may find our map is outdated or we don't have the right equipment. Roads may be blocked, and we may need to backtrack to find a clear route.

The journey to connect with your Higher Self can also have its obstacles. We have established beliefs and conditioning that can make it difficult to synch up with the Higher Self.

Though we are an aspect of our Higher Self, it operates in a field of much higher frequency than what we experience in the third-dimensional realm of the human form. Synching up, therefore, requires raising the vibrational frequency of the human form to more closely match this higher expression and sustain it in everyday life as much as possible. While we may have moments of experiencing a higher vibration, we typically drop back down to a lower-frequency vibration by default. Aligning with our Higher Self and incorporating that high vibration fully into our being is required for true, lasting spiritual evolution.

One way to conceptualize how vibrational frequency works in the human body is by analogy to an electrical appliance that requires compatible voltage to function correctly. Consider, for example, what happens when an American-made 120-watt hairdryer is plugged into an electrical socket in England that runs a 220-watt electrical current. The motor quickly burns out, and the hairdryer is ruined because it receives more electricity than it can handle. However, savvy travelers know that using a simple converter adjusts the flow of electricity so the hairdryer motor doesn't get overloaded.

Having lived in England and Italy, I thought I was well-versed in electrical differences and the adjustments needed to accommodate them. However, the lesson clearly wasn't fully integrated until I was trying to resolve a problem with a hallway light constantly going out in my home in Italy. Each time I replaced the bulb, it would illuminate for a few minutes, then fry out and pop. I was convinced we had an electrical problem and requested an electrician assess the situation. The electrician fiddled around with the light fixture and wiring but didn't see anything obviously wrong. Finally, he looked at the lightbulb and noticed the English writing on it. There it was. Even with all my travel experience, it never occurred to me that the 120-watt lightbulbs packed up with all our other worldly possessions in the transfer of our lives from one side of the Atlantic to the other would blow out with 220-watt voltage. Through these sacrificial lightbulbs, I learned firsthand the crucial lesson that whatever receives power must be properly equipped to handle its strength.

Energetically, the human body also has a unique frequency, and we can experience disorientation or discomfort if we receive energy incompatible with our *wattage*. When trying to make a conscious connection with our Higher Self, we may feel like the 120-watt hairdryer or light bulb connected to a 220-watt socket and get an uncomfortable zap from the experience. Fortunately, like the savvy traveler, spiritual travelers also have tools for adjusting the difference in frequency between our human body and Higher Self, making the flow of energy seamless.

The high-frequency energy of your Higher Self is a very real energy that is available to flow to you. When your body is attuned to a lower frequency, it is not compatible with an influx of higher-frequency energies. It can be too much, too fast. A quick and sudden surge of spiritual power might seem desirable to a spiritual seeker. However, the powerful energy surge can damage one's mind-body-spirit complex or overload the nervous system if one is unprepared for the experience. Patience, wisdom, and trust are required when attempting to bring higher frequencies into your human form to avoid overload. Joseph Campbell summed this up perfectly in this metaphor: *the mystic swims happily in the same water that drowns a madman.*[2]

RECOGNIZING LOW-FREQUENCY PATTERNS AND INFLUENCES

Generating a vibrational frequency compatible with our Higher Self requires realizing where we may be running low-frequency energy, which makes us ill-equipped to receive and hold the high-frequency energy needed to commune with higher consciousness. Identifying the source of persistent low-frequency patterns can reveal energy blocks that prevent connection with our Higher Self. These energy blocks develop within us for many reasons, some of which are due simply to being on Earth at this time, which we explore deeply in this chapter. Other reasons are due to specific choices we make that are not aligned with a higher level of consciousness, such as ignoring opportunities for experiences, relationships/friendships, studies, or jobs that would be nurturing for our souls.

Focusing on what really matters from a higher perspective is key to aligning with the higher-frequency energy at a soul level. Diverting attention to what authority figures deem important instead of what is innately important to us takes us out of soul alignment. This misalignment leads to discontentment, dissatisfaction, and a lack of fulfillment.

Discovering what is innately important requires a journey of self-discovery, just like knowing yourself as a soul and connecting to your Higher Self takes work and dedication. Quieting your mind, examining and working on your triggers, shining light onto your shadows, and more are required to know what drives you, lights your fire, and brings you fulfillment. From that point, you can start to focus your thoughts, words, and activities on what matters to you, allowing you to build your life with purpose and overcome low-energy blocks and patterns.

In this chapter, we'll examine some common ways you may be unintentionally maintaining a lower vibrational frequency that prevents you from connecting with the higher vibrational energy necessary for expanding consciousness and connecting with your Higher Self. In the next chapter, we'll explore practical ways to raise your vibrational frequency to break through energy blocks and reach your highest energetic potential.

FAMILY MATTERS

The energetic imprint left by our childhood family is a major influence on our habits, attitudes, and outlook on life, which can significantly affect our vibrational frequency. The early conditioning we receive from the environment of our upbringing permeates our current life and colors our life experiences so strongly that its influence can be difficult to recognize. These ingrained patterns can be such a part of our character that we may never pause to consider if there are other ways to be.

Lower vibrational tendencies expressed in your current life can come from learned behaviors you were exposed to in your childhood family. Your early years were very much shaped by your early caregivers. They determined what you ate, when you slept, what you wore, whether you had pets, if or where you went on vacation, if you could go out to play and with whom, and every other detail of your early life. Family behavior related to alcohol or drug use, sex, anger, manipulation, victimization, power, co-dependency, and much more also had an impact on your energetic makeup.

Through the decisions of your parents and caregivers, you learned how life worked. Your parents' reactions taught you what was acceptable or not. How they reacted to you and others imprinted you with ideas about right and wrong behavior that may still influence you as an adult.

All in Due Time

A good example of how familial patterns relate to our vibrational frequency is our relationship with time. For some, the relationship with time is a higher-vibrational experience of ease and flow; for others, it's a lower-vibrational experience of stress and control. I'm drawn to this example of how we are impacted by time for a couple of reasons. First, time is benign. Many people experienced painful traumas from within their family during early childhood, which shapes their life experience and vibrational frequency to this day. While using traumatic examples stemming from child abuse, alcohol abuse, sexual trauma, and so forth would be powerful, I don't see value in picking wounds like those for our purposes here.

Second, time is a universal experience for all humans. Someone could have had a very loving childhood without a whisper of trauma and mistakenly conclude they have no lasting vibrational imprint from their upbringing. Conversely, because no one eludes the pervasiveness of time, it can be a useful approach to unearthing the hidden ways our upbringing can still be pulling the strings in our lives.

On one end of the spectrum of lower-vibrational relationships with time is strict adherence to a schedule, and on the other, a disregard for time altogether. Both extremes create stress for you and others that can be felt in your energy body and radiate out in your energy field. Those who are very deliberate and conscientious about time may get overly stressed about being late or overly sensitive when others are late. They work hard to ensure they are always on time and get frustrated or angry when others are late. They may equate being late with being disrespectful or disrespected. All of these experiences with time invoke a lower vibrational state. Because time is an undercurrent of everyday life, these thoughts and beliefs about being late may frequently pull down their vibration.

Those on the other side of the spectrum have only a vague sense of time. They may view planning to meet at a certain time as a rough approximation, and arriving anywhere within an hour of that time is close enough. They may never consider how the other parties involved have adjusted their day to be present at the agreed time or how they could damage the plans immediately following that meeting, which will need to be pushed back due to their inattentiveness. For some, there is a subconscious, hidden part that derives a sense of pleasure in controlling others by being tardy. They might even use being late as a power play to imply that the planned engagement wasn't a priority, minimizing its importance and the value of those attending. While they may not experience the direct stress that comes from the other end of the spectrum, these unhealthy behaviors strain relationships and, thus, indirectly cause a lower-frequency vibration through the undesirable fallouts of not taking others into account. Additionally, the habitual prioritization of themselves over others hints at a lower vibrational state of consciousness.

In many cases, our attitudes and beliefs about time were imprinted on us by our parents' behaviors. We picked up the energetic response of our caretakers when they were dealing with punctuality issues and subconsciously adopted their behaviors and reactions.

Time is such a foundational factor of our human experience that we are nearly oblivious to our relationship to it. We don't step back and consider that our worth is not tied to a clock. Whether we must be on time at all costs, prefer to keep people waiting, or interact with time somewhere in between, our behavior may be based on a pattern passed on through our family. If the imprint from our upbringing is holding us in a lower vibrational pattern, this awareness helps us to neutralize our thoughts and break the lower vibrational cycle.

If you recognize that you are in a low-frequency relationship to time that is negatively impacting your vibrational frequency, there are actions you can take to shift out of these patterns. Just because you've carried these beliefs for as long as you can remember does not mean you are powerless to reshape them. Understand that life is fluid, with many factors at play beyond your immediate concerns. You can strive to be on time for engagements without letting the desire for punctuality cause stress, make you drive dangerously, or induce feelings of shame. Similarly, you can choose to be slow to take offense when you are kept waiting, remembering that others have a fluid life, too, and offering them grace.

Alternatively, if you have a pattern of being late, consider the impact and undertones of the subtle message you send to those you keep waiting. Reflect on whether you have picked up generational habits of controlling and overpowering others and whether your behavior regarding time is a facet of that tendency.

Generational Cycles

Generational cycles of familial patterns and energy imprints can greatly impact our vibrational frequency. The example of how generational cycles can influence our relationship to time and punctuality is somewhat benign, but there are many other aspects of these imprints that can result in much more damaging subconscious lower-frequency patterns.

We were born to parents with familial imprints, who themselves were born to parents with familial imprints, and on and on. Each parent in that generational cycle carried a huge energy imprint from their early childhood that influenced the vibrational bandwidth they passed on to their children. So, while it can be easy to point the finger at parents for the cycle of patterns and imprints they may have perpetuated, we can equally extend compassion for what they endured and potentially overcame to get them to where they are.

When exploring the influence of generational cycles in our own lives, become aware of family vibrational patterns not to assign blame but to realize that beliefs can be mistaken for factual truth about ourselves and the world. These beliefs can disempower us from making changes that bring us closer to connecting with our Higher Self.

Beliefs we've carried our whole lives run deep because they have been present from the start, shaping our attitudes, thoughts, words, and actions. How we speak to our partners, the importance we place on work, our political views, and how we care for our health are all examples of influence from family patterns. We may never question these beliefs because they feel core to our identity and seem irrefutable.

Be aware that generational habits and programming may not always be healthy. They can keep us in a low-frequency vibration, subconsciously perpetuating behaviors that prevent us from expressing our highest vibration and communicating with our Higher Self.

Media Madness and Fear

In our pursuit of being informed and concerned citizens, we can inadvertently hold ourselves in a low frequency of fear. We give away our personal power and remain disconnected from our Higher Selves through our addiction to media— TV, news, advertisements, social media, movies, books, magazines, and video games. These distractions work together to capture our attention and influence us to fall further and further into fear, anger, stress, and separation. If we are not using conscious discernment in our media consumption, we risk mindlessly being told what to think, say, wear, like, dislike, and particularly what to worry about.

Be very careful about what you set your precious eyeballs on because what you are taking in is subtly but very powerfully shaping you. Big tech and advertising companies invest huge amounts of time, research, and money into understanding human psychology. They use their intel about subconscious human behavior to keep you sucked into whatever they are selling, from products to ideas. If you desire to connect more deeply with your Higher Self, being pulled into the latest news, trends, and entertainment can divert your attention away from reaching your goal. Your precious time, energy, and attention spent on distraction is time lost from going inward and doing the work that will give you access to higher consciousness. Changing your relationship with media makes a difference in so many ways. Removing its influence is an effective way to open a channel to your Higher Self.

News media will *always* have a fresh crisis for you to worry about. This constant barrage of one emergency after the other keeps us addicted to staying tuned in to find out what we should be worried about and perpetuates fear within us. Subconsciously, we want to know about the breaking news because we believe being informed keeps us safe. But if we consider that news agencies are deliberately selling fear to build viewership, translating into myriad financial benefits, we begin to realize how habitually engaging in news media keeps us addicted to being in a state of fear. Fortunately, we have choice and can simply stop feeding ourselves a steady diet of media influences screaming at us about all the things we should be worried about and, instead, turn our attention to thoughts, activities, and people that don't foster fear.

Diluting Your Personal Power

Key to this realization is a profound awareness that there is only so much time each day to engage with life. The more you engage with and focus on something, the stronger the imprint it will have on your life. Mastery of anything, even expanding your consciousness, results from focused attention over a prolonged period. If you want to become a master violinist, you must spend hours upon hours playing the violin. That time you spend playing violin is at the expense of doing other things. You can spend a couple of hours a week on your violin and become good at it. If you play for a couple of hours a day, you will know your violin much better and will be noticeably more adept than someone who spends two hours per week playing. If you spend most of your day playing violin, day after day, you will have a *much* more nuanced understanding of the instrument and be quite proficient in the subtle ways you can be in flow with it. Dedicating a large portion of your waking hours to playing the violin will take your music from something you know the mechanics of doing to something you create with a greater part of yourself. You can feel yourself becoming one with the violin, merging with it, riding a wave of creation together. Getting to that level of mastery takes time, focus, and dedication.

Reaching higher states of consciousness that open you up to connection with the Higher Self requires operating from a state of empowerment. Your personal power comes from your ability to focus your energy. When you are distracted, your thoughts and energy are scattered and diffused. Consider the difference between filtered light and a laser pointer. Filtered light is spread out and subtle. A laser is so concentrated that it can cut through or burn things. Like filtered light, when you are not focusing your attention, your energy is scattered and not very powerful. Becoming intentional and increasing your ability to focus allows your energy to coalesce onto one thing, increasing its power like a laser. In today's world, where you are constantly bombarded with fears, triggers, and advertisements from the media as you scroll or tune into broadcasted programming, your attention is easily scattered.

When we focus on media as a significant influence in our lives, we are pulling our attention and energy away from what truly has meaning in our lives, whether mastering the violin or mastering how we live life, and diverting it to external noise and distraction. This opens the door to outside forces that are not the least bit concerned with our desire to connect with our Higher Self, telling us what is important, what we should think about, and what to do. Through our constant attention to media, we surrender our personal power and sovereignty to someone else's agenda. These hidden agendas thrive on us remaining in a lower vibrational frequency, preventing us from fully realizing our personal power.

Revealing Hidden Treasures

Disengaging with media reveals some amazing gold nuggets. The first is time. Media is a complete time suck. I shudder to think of all the hours I spent scrolling through news articles or my Facebook newsfeed. Regrettably, much of that scrolling happened while I was with my kids when they were playing. My eyes were glued to my phone while they ran around laughing and growing up in front of me. I know how it feels to perceive staying up to date with the news cycle as an accomplishment. Remember, media companies study human behavior and deliberately design apps, games, and TV programs to exploit our natural tendencies.

The second gold nugget is the clearing of all that energetic noise. Our energetic fields are unable to remain calm and smooth while bombarded with the media's constant input. The metaphorical noise of the media machine pulls down our vibrational frequency. The media often causes us to feel fear, anger, unworthiness, jealousy, separation, and judgment. These types of emotional responses keep us glued to the media, searching for the very security that it is siphoning from us. On some level, we expect that the solution to the fear we feel from the news story exists within the news cycle. However, as Einstein wisely observed, problems are not solved by the same level of consciousness that created them. To get to a higher level of consciousness, we need to get out of what keeps us stuck in a lower one. The media is a major culprit in keeping people trapped in a lower level of consciousness.

I stopped watching and scrolling through the news a while ago and have been ever grateful for the enormous benefit of cutting out the constant worry and fear from media overexposure. My mind is freer without the clutter of distractions from information that doesn't support my spiritual progress. I spend very little, if any, time in fear, as I am not allowing an onslaught of fear-based stories to take my attention. I don't miss important world events because I inevitably hear about any stories with enough momentum from the masses. I have been able to reinvest hours of time I used to spend on social and traditional media into my connection with my Higher Self.

In these times of polarized views, be mindful of how others may view the choice to disengage with certain media, especially news media. Many people may not relate to your decision and feel provoked by your not staying abreast of the news. Particularly if you are new to disengaging from the influence of the media, sharing your choice with others may be a more challenging discussion than you intend.

People with a mainstream mentality can be very entrenched in the illusion of the value of the media and resistant to views that challenge that notion. They feel the media keeps them informed and conclude that people who avoid the media are woefully ignorant, out of touch, and choosing to keep their heads in the sand. It's important for you to be ok with that. Respect their choice in the same way you would hope they will respect yours. They haven't considered how they hand over their energy and power through this entanglement with the media. That gateway of understanding is still out on the horizon for them, and depending on their life's journey, they may pass through it in their own time, or they may choose to remain under that outside influence throughout their lifetime. Their path is their own. Your job is to understand what you are being called to do with your life, what is the highest and best good for you, and to overcome your need for validation by expecting other people in your life to go through the same gateway of understanding as you at the same time.

Standing by choices such as untangling from the media because they are the right decisions for you and who you are becoming is of utmost importance. Be comfortable making changes that align you with a higher vibration, even if you don't see your friends, family, colleagues, and neighbors doing likewise.

If you haven't already started pulling away from the news and distracting social media, try it and see how you feel. If you are already moving in that direction, take a bigger step, creating a greater distance between you and these distracting and manipulative influences. Give yourself time to get used to it. At first, you may feel a little lost or out of touch. Removing something from your routine can create the sense of a vacuum where you feel like something is missing. The vacuum left by removing media from your life will be compounded by the fact that many people in your world will likely remain engaged with it. Topics will certainly come up during the day that friends and family expect you will have seen in the news and have opinions about.

You can become comfortable saying, "That hasn't made it on my radar yet."

They can then tell you about the current event if you wish, or you might instead find something else to talk about.

With spiritual maturity, you require less validation from others. You do not need to convince anyone else that you are doing the right thing; you know within yourself what is true for you, even if you are not seeing the same choices reflected by the people around you. Adopt the neutral *you do you* mentality. The reality at this time is that if you are making changes to raise your vibration, you will be outpacing the spiritual growth of the mainstream masses. Focusing on spiritual growth is simply not a priority for most people. In fact, for many, it doesn't even cross their minds. Get comfortable standing confidently in unconventional decisions for yourself.

SCHOOL DAZE

Throughout childhood, what we are taught in school has a major influence on the programming of our thoughts and beliefs, which influences our vibration. To give context to my perspective, I attended public schools and universities, and my kids have attended both public and private schools. As a product of the traditional system, I took the way school is run for granted for a long time.

Of course, attending school and receiving a traditional education has important benefits, not the least of which is that it simply paves the way for us to be productive in society. Leaving home to go to school is one of the first ways we start to experience life outside of our family and assert some autonomy. Especially if life at home was a confusing minefield where it was difficult to connect with family members, perhaps school life offered a reprieve through feeling accepted by a teacher, finding a supportive friend group, or taking comfort in the predictability of math.

With the total acceptance of school as a social benefit and absolute necessity, we may never stop to consider if the structure of the traditional school system is creating the optimal human experience. Despite the benefits of conventional schooling, it is another place where we are shaped and conditioned in accordance with an outside agenda. We are taught and tested on what our teachers value based on the dictates of a state-approved curriculum. My observation is that students are funneled into a largely outdated system that values the sciences and economic productivity over creative and liberal arts studies.

The education machine is largely designed to produce a workforce that will continue to fuel the industrialized corporate complex. Success in terms of academic achievement means honing a skill set that will earn money in exchange for keeping the industrial-corporate mega system thriving. Unfortunately, this kind of success requires spending the majority of the life experience economically and psychologically trapped as a metaphorical cog in the wheel. Obedience and compliance are drilled in, stifling creativity, personal sovereignty, and self-empowerment.

This complete desensitization to creativity and self-expression is a tremendous obstacle to connecting with your Higher Self, especially when we consider that traditional schooling is completely devoid of any framework of spirituality. Rather, school curriculums are solely based on understanding the physical, material world, with no mention of the role of consciousness in how the world works.

What We Are Not Taught

I am fascinated by studies illustrating that consciousness influences the physical world in ways we are not taught in school. This research highlights the vast, untapped potential within humans to utilize the energy within us. Caroline Cory's stunning film documentaries *Superhuman: The Invisible Made Visible* and *Among Us* beautifully illustrate the role of consciousness and the untapped potential of humans.[3] In these films, Cory executes many fascinating experiments with highly esteemed scientists that show the power of our consciousness in affecting change and receiving intel. She investigates remote viewing and telekinesis, influencing the alkalinity of DNA through focused intention, accurately *seeing* without sight, and many more examples that defy the laws of Newtonian physics and reality as we understand them.

The extraordinary skills displayed in these films can be learned and become part of the average human experience. Indeed, these films show several instances of people who have never been exposed to training their superpower, achieving remarkable results quickly. The point is not that some extraordinary people are gifted with these phenomenal abilities but that the skills can be learned and honed with practice.

I find it particularly revealing about where we are on our evolutionary path to see that there is little, if any, exposure to consciousness and spirituality in primary and secondary-level schooling, even though we are spiritual beings. Imagine if part of our schooling was nurturing our consciousness to truly know and experience the phenomenal power within each of us. Students could be learning about what mystics through the ages have been teaching about the workings of the Universe and the nature of reality. They could be learning advanced breathwork practices to facilitate their experiences of expanded consciousness. They could be exploring the coding within the works of Shakespeare and the Bible, sacred geometry, or mathematics related to the Fibonacci sequence seen throughout nature. They could be learning how our biology and emotions respond to sound, vibration, and color.

There are so many mysteries we have hidden away in this world that could be explored during those tender years when we are ripe for learning, which would radically change our human experience if the masses had exposure to them the way they do to the content of traditional schooling. Instead, the school experience focuses nearly exclusively on mental acuity and often represses inherent gifts. With a strictly mainstream school experience, we are largely focused on things that don't expose and nurture the greatness within us. We aren't encouraged to discover our unique gifts or how we can live our lives according to our purpose.

At this time in humanity, if we want to raise our vibration and expand our consciousness to become the highest version of ourselves, we must do so on our own time. More often than not, we must actually unlearn the limiting beliefs we have received through traditional education about how the world works and our place within it.

I am confident that there are people dedicated to creating a school system tailored to developing conscious awareness in children and nurturing their connection to higher levels of consciousness. I can easily see that being part of society in the future, shaped by people with the necessary gifts, talents, and passions to manifest that reality. Their vision will transform education from rote memorization and grooming for becoming cogs in the corporate machine to nurturing an understanding of the role of consciousness, teaching students how to experience themselves as energy, reach higher levels of consciousness for their highest good and be a benefit to all.

HIGH SOCIETY – OR FRIENDS IN LOW PLACES?

Next on the list of usual suspects keeping us in a low-frequency vibration is society and social structure, otherwise known as collective consciousness. Observing and interacting with our peer groups and how we see others behaving in public influences our own thoughts, ideas, and behaviors.

The largest cohesive societal collectives tend to be based on nationality. But there are also societal collectives with global reach based on religious beliefs, race, gender, economic status, and education. Conversely, more localized expressions of societal influence can come from a city, community, neighborhood, or group association. The societal pressures, perspectives, and expectations can vary greatly from group to group. For example, the societal parameters around a member of an Amish community will be very different from those of a Fortune 500 executive. Still, the imprint of their respective sub-society will be enormous to each of them personally.

Based on the societies we are exposed to, there is a tendency to unquestioningly assume that the opinions, thoughts, and actions about how things are done within our groups are the right way, especially if we grew up in the same sub-societies that we are part of in adulthood.

Societal influence echoes all throughout your day. The hot topics that everyone is talking about are constantly changing, and rarely, if ever, are they issues that lead us into higher frequency thought. These trending topics feel like the most important thing in the world because they are continuously reinforced through your daily discussions. Typically, these matters stem from what the media is drilling into us, which bleeds into conversations with friends, at the water cooler at work, and around the dinner table. Some trending topics that took root in society in this century are terrorism, gender equality, racism, and vaccinations. In America, we also see the flare-up of much of our attention going toward one societal issue every four years when the election circus begins, and we go even deeper into divisiveness. The deeper we go into the weeds of picking a side, defending our viewpoint, and shaming others with a different opinion, the more we reinforce lower frequencies of thought.

These trending topics float in the collective consciousness and make their way to most people, even if they intentionally avoid the news. We have even gotten to the point where we so carefully police our language that we feel forced to repress ourselves for fear of appearing to be unsympathetic. People learn to toe the popular line lest they be *canceled*. We see this happening on the main stage with celebrities. But it also happens in smaller pockets within communities, as people turn their backs on those whose conversational flow has not been sanitized thoroughly enough. We constantly learn what society wants us to think, reflect that in our speech, and then condemn and turn our backs on those not adopting those beliefs. These low-frequency fears of being ostracized hold us in a lower vibrational pattern. We close ourselves to the natural flow of organic and original thinking in order to stay within the boundaries set forth by the community. We parrot each other to continuously reflect what is socially comfortable, even when new understandings, thoughts, and ideas could spiral us upward into higher levels of awareness, where we more easily connect to the Higher Self.

Some people are more susceptible to societal influence and peer pressure than others. I remember when my son was a toddler, someone suggested I influence him by pointing out examples of good behavior.

This was supposed to be something like, "Look, Johnny is eating his peas! You'll like them, too!"

When I tried this, my son looked at me like I had just come from another planet. *What does Johnny's taste in peas have to do with me?* His eyes seemed to ask.

He was never motivated by mimicking what others liked or

were doing. I hope that this quality will stay with him. Staying aligned with what is important to him versus what is popular will indeed serve him well.

For those who are very drawn to eating their peas, following Johnny's example, extra mindfulness and diligence will be required to distinguish what is truly important to them, such as Higher Self connection, from the societal influence clogging up the collective energy field.

Keeping up with what society deems important in the day-to-day is a lot of work. Imagine if you decided not to let society determine what you value. You weren't afraid to have no strong opinion about the push-pull, us-vs-them topic du jour. Instead of utilizing your time and energy to stay current on what is acceptable or interesting by the standards of your peers, you focus on quieting your mind, strengthening your connection to your Higher Self, understanding your role and purpose for this life, examining and working on your triggers and shadows, and doing other work to sculpt yourself into your highest version. If you really focused on those activities and redirected the time spent keeping up with society toward connecting with your inner world, you could be a completely different person.

INTERWEAVING FACTORS COMPLETE THE PICTURE

Of course, nothing exists in a bubble, and all the factors we have explored influence each other. A family environment that is heavily penetrated by the news media leads to behaviors and conversations within the household that reflect trending crises. Family time influences behavior at school and in society. The behaviors learned from friends and influences from teachers are brought home, affecting family dynamics.

You are a member of each of these areas of influence, and the more you step into being aligned to a higher vibration, the more you are capable of being a force of influence within your environment. Think of your entire being as one creation and consider each area of influence discussed in this chapter as making up a percentage of your being. Perhaps at this point in your life, 50% of your thoughts and behaviors are subconsciously coming from your family upbringing, 25% from media, 10% from schooling, 10% from society, and 5% from your independent personal choices.

As you go through the process of connecting to your soul and Higher Self, you become more aware of the thoughts and behaviors that are obstacles to your Higher Self connection. As these obstacles become visible to you, you can begin to see their origins. Simply by becoming aware of what keeps you from reaching a higher vibration, you are empowered to mindfully make new, higher vibrational choices aligned with your soul. The influence of low-frequency vibrational imprints from family, media, school, and social consciousness decreases. You can let go of the lower vibrational patterns, invite new thoughts and behaviors, and create new choices. Over time, as the subconscious patterns from these outside factors become less influential, your own independent personal choices increase in percentage. The energetic power you reclaim through decreasing outside influence and being aligned with your Higher Self is very real, and your vibration is more influential in your surrounding environment.

We are constantly intermixing, observing, and adjusting dynamically to our environment. We test things out, try things on, and see if different ideas, thoughts, and behaviors benefit our lives. Bringing our conscious awareness to the external influences that keep us locked in a lower vibration can help us reveal what supports our connection to our Higher Self. Through our awareness, we have less and less subconscious and involuntary influence streaming into our lives and more freedom to become greater versions of ourselves through access to higher levels of consciousness.

Take the first step toward reclaiming your attention by having a media fast! Remove all notifications from all news outlets on your phone. Decide if you want to tackle the news outlets, social media, or both. With the notifications turned off, you won't be interrupted throughout the day by what someone else has deemed important or *like* notices racking up on a post.

Next, take it a step further and don't open the apps during downtime.

Plan ahead for some other things you can do when you would normally be munching on the news or social media. You could instead breathe deeply into your belly. Feel your belly extend outward as it fills with breath, and then feel it relax back toward your spine as you exhale. You can count these slow breaths and use this as a focal point to take your attention away from the attraction to checking media. Notice how you feel after five breaths.

I also encourage you to track your media fast progress in a journal. This serves two purposes. It allows you to reflect on what you notice from your media fast and organize your thoughts about it. It also gives you something to do with the time that you were filling with media consumption.

Here are some journaling ideas:

- What are you doing with the time you've gotten back?

- How do you feel being less connected to media?

- If staying off media is challenging, is it getting harder or easier as you push forward with your media fast?

- What else is coming up for you as you listen to your inner voice free from distraction?

Let yourself dry out from your media intake. Find an approach that works with your personality type. Some people prefer to go cold turkey and completely remove media temptations, while others prefer to gradually decrease their media intake. Try removing completely or dramatically decreasing the time you spend on media and notice the results. Whatever path you choose, celebrate your victories, whether they are hours or days of reclaimed time.

CHAPTER 3

BEFRIENDING THE HIGHER SELF

Imagine you are traveling in an unfamiliar place. You are checking your map, trying to orient yourself with the street names around you. You aren't sure of the best direction to go or even which sites you would enjoy the most. Just as you are starting to feel overwhelmed, a guide appears from the crowd and comes straight to you. She smiles, calmly places her hand on your shoulder, and points confidently in the direction you will most enjoy. You understand that this guide has your best interests at heart. She knows precisely why you are in this place, your deepest desire in being here, and how your presence satisfies your needs and the needs of those you will encounter. How much more optimized might your experience be by having such a special guide?

Now imagine that you have access to such a guide not only while you travel in an unfamiliar place but also as you move through each moment of your life. Your Higher Self knows the lessons you came to learn, the things you came to experience, who around you holds the key to the next best opportunity, and what pitfalls are down the road. Befriending your Higher Self empowers you to maneuver more easily and confidently as you travel your path.

In the last chapter, we explored how the modern human experience stands in the way of connecting with your Higher Self. Let's change our focus now to the other side of the coin. What are some ways to strengthen your connection to your Higher Self?

Limitless opportunities can await you when you take steps to integrate higher vibrational energies. You can reach new heights and have experiences you may think are reserved for elite spiritual adepts, such as monks or shamans.

MY PERSONAL MULTIDIMENSIONAL JOURNEYS

Through my dedication to bringing more of my Higher Self into my human existence, I have had some truly fantastical and mystical experiences that are profound and impactful in my life, including seeing energy patterns, receiving multifaceted intuitive insights, feeling vibrations, hearing tones, and seeing lights. These experiences are extraordinary gifts that light me up.

Most of these mystical, multidimensional experiences happen as I drift off to sleep. Instead of falling asleep, I start seeing visual input behind my closed eyes, which is very different from the visions in a dream state. These visuals often include specific patterns, geometry, colors, and symbols. I rarely perceive beings or landscapes; typically, there is no story or plot. I also receive auditory input, which can sound like an unfamiliar spoken language. What I see and hear is unfamiliar to my everyday human experience, and I am unaware of a being or consciousness giving explanations. As a new understanding or insight enters my thoughts, I have an all-pervasive knowing of hidden truths revealed.

Because we don't have a common language to draw from for these nebulous events, they are difficult to explain. Perhaps a good starting point is to describe what it looks like behind my closed eyes during everyday waking consciousness. Although you might think it would be totally black, what I see is kind of staticky looking. Similar to how old TV sets look when they aren't picking up a channel, I see tiny, fuzzy, chaotic spots of light constantly jumping around behind my closed eyes.

Inner Sights, Sounds, and Feelings

During my multidimensional experiences, the chaotic, staticky visuals give way and organize into shapes, repeating patterns, colors, and light. Instead of the static, it may look like I am inside a beautiful dome decorated with intricate mosaic patterns. I often sense that I am inside a gorgeous mosque, even though I have no human experience of being in a mosque. Alternatively, the static can become a long hallway with an arched ceiling and columns down the sides, the whole scene made of repeating and constantly moving patterns and colors. The sense reminds me of a cathedral or abbey with stained glass.

Often, the visual phenomena are accompanied by vibrations in my body. These physical vibrating sensations are usually associated with one chakra at a time. Sometimes one chakra will vibrate for a while, then stop, and another will start. Other times, I will have one part of my body vibrating that is more isolated than where the major chakras are located, such as one foot up to my calf.

The sounds I hear can be like a hum, ringing, bells, and sometimes like language—either English or one I don't know. The voice I hear can be either male or female. On two occasions, I heard the voice say a day of the week, a month, and a date. I wrote down the information and was amazed to find that the date did fall on the day of the given week. Both times, the date I heard had no previous relevance to me and was too far in the future for me to mentally calculate the day of the week it would land on. In those instances, when the date arrived weeks later, nothing earth-shattering happened in the outside world. However, I had what seemed to be upgrades to my consciousness in my inner world. For instance, in an upcoming chapter, The Heart Gateway, I share about a sensation in my heart associated with phasing into a higher frequency, which caused me to pull my car over as I was driving. I had heard the day and date of that experience in advance.

Kaleidoscope of Mirrors

As I mentioned, sometimes there is also a *knowing* that comes through from these experiences, even though there doesn't seem to be the presence of an individuated being communicating this information to me. An experience of a sudden knowing that I had involved seeing repeating patterns that turned into mirrors reflecting fractal shapes that were constantly changing. It reminded me of looking into a kaleidoscope, with its mirrored reflections making symmetrical, continually evolving designs. Immediately, I knew—without knowing *how* I knew—that these complex mirrored fractal designs represented everything I consider external to myself that always reflects back to me.

Like the kaleidoscope, these mirrors constantly change and adjust, adapting what I see based on my own thoughts about what I am observing. I understood that when I look at another person, I don't see a pure, true representation of them. I see a complex amalgamation of mirrors reflecting back to me what I am focusing on about them at that moment, and that reflection is actually reflecting my own state of mind back to me.

Multifaceted Solution

The experience of knowing that what I see in the external world is truly reflecting me back to myself in a metaphorical kaleidoscope of mirrors expanded me into a broader understanding of the nature of reality. I have also experienced instantaneous knowings that are less generally philosophical and more specifically related to a problem I am trying to solve.

At a certain point in writing the very book you are holding right at this moment—*hello to you in what is my future as I write this, from me in what is your past as you read it*—I had to choose between investing in an editor or self-publishing without professional assistance. My earnings as a spiritual teacher and podcast host are much more lucrative in the sense-of-personal-fulfillment category than the financial one, so I didn't have enough funds to cover an editor in my little business account. I felt that having an editor was important, and to cover the cost, I considered different options like dipping into my retirement fund from my corporate days or getting a loan from the bank.

I was in this conundrum for a while when I finally saw the situation from a much higher perspective during one of my nighttime multidimensional experiences. I was seeing lights and patterns and feeling different vibrations. The unfolding patterns appeared to be some kind of code my human mind could not consciously decipher, but a deeper part of me could receive and understand. All at once, I had a complete knowing of many facets of my problem and how the solution had the potential to work through many layers of my life, offering several soul gifts all at once. I was in awe at the brilliance.

The solution I received in this multidimensional state was to ask someone in my life to invest in me by covering the editor's fees. I could clearly see four main ways this solution would benefit us both.

- Although an exceptionally good person by any standards, they are not actively pursuing spiritual growth at this time, and investing in this book was a way for them to use their resources to nurture their spiritual side on an unconscious level. By saying yes to this project, they were saying yes to their own spiritual expansion, even though making an investment in this book may not outwardly seem directly related to spirituality, as we might understand it.

- I also saw that one of my shadows is my pride, which I hadn't really noticed before. I can be independent to a fault, and allowing my soul to expand into graciously receiving help from others is an important area of spiritual growth.

- Because it is very uncomfortable for me to surrender to dependence, I needed to tap into my courage and strength so I could do this thing that needed to be done but made me very uncomfortable—*ask for help.*

- As hard as it would be, I also knew that my asking would bring us closer. They would appreciate my honesty, vulnerability, and trust in them to help me.

These insights were revealed to me all at once. It appeared to me as a magnificent, intelligent design. I knew that I had many options to choose from, but ultimately, this was the highest solution for the greatest good from a soul level. To tell you just how deep that pride shadow goes, even having that profound insight and seeing how asking for the money in this personal relationship was a soul-win for all involved, I *still* was so nervous that I cried from the discomfort and had to ask over email to keep my thoughts straight.

By following the insights from that multidimensional experience, I did indeed find that it was a soul-win for all. They said yes without hesitation and also had some ideas I hadn't thought of regarding how I had things set up for my business from a tax perspective.

My little Kara human self lacks the omnipotent nature necessary to weave such an intricate tapestry of opportunities for growth in so many different facets of life. That particular multidimensional experience helped me see clearer than ever that a divine dance is moving through our lives, opening up possibilities through our challenges that are, by default, hidden from our conscious awareness.

Each multidimensional experience has reinforced my connection with my Higher Self and the realms beyond our physical world. However, much more often, the signals and communication I receive are more subtle but still incredibly valuable in my everyday living.

There are many ways we can engage more directly with the intelligent consciousness of the Higher Self and recognize its guidance and communication. Let's explore some helpful tools for opening up to this magical, expansive, and transformative connection.

FINDING YOUR CENTER WITH MEDITATION

Meditation has been a huge game changer for me in connecting with my Higher Self. Taking time each day to be still and feel into my soul reinforces the spiritual perspective that takes the weight off of inevitable challenges in the material world. Regularly tuning into my Higher Self through meditation has allowed me to strengthen my ability to perceive subtle energy, which has greatly strengthened my intuition.

Don't discount the importance of meditation. I know you're busy. You have a lot of demands, and you feel stretched thin. Sitting still and not *doing* anything may not feel like the best use of your time. But having a clear inner space for open connection with your Higher Self is the most direct way to reach higher levels of consciousness.

What You Get

Meditation is simply a quieting of the mind that allows us to perceive the subtle messages and nudges from our inner knowing. Through meditation, we disconnect from the details of daily life to fill our being with calmness and peace. I gain the most benefit from meditation by practicing every single day. Meditation has a cumulative effect. There are measurable, beneficial changes to the brain and nervous system from continued practice. The more you do it, the more it changes you. Studies show that in as little as eight weeks, the prefrontal cortex thickens from just 12-15 minutes of meditation per day. [4] The prefrontal cortex is where you experience calmness and emotional regulation. A strong prefrontal cortex invokes greater joy in your life while quieting the part of your brain that is associated with fear and anger.

Beyond the effects of calmness and emotional regulation, meditation is a quintessential tool for communicating with your Higher Self and accessing parts of yourself beyond your human self, personality, and ego. Through stilling the thoughts in meditation, you gradually get to know the feeling and resonance of your soul and begin to discern if inspiration is coming from a place of higher consciousness or if it is the egoic consciousness. Shifting from the perspective of the little self to Higher Self doesn't require going deep into a trance state or anything complicated. Simply getting used to being still and learning to quiet your thoughts helps you access untapped places within.

Whispering Guidance of the Soul

You can train yourself to cut through the noise of modern life by consistently and intentionally taking time to quiet your thoughts and tune into your inner world. Once you get used to stilling your thoughts, you can explore directing your attention to tune into your soul. With focus, you can learn to decipher the subtle clues, keys, and messages you get from higher levels of consciousness through your energy.

Meditation can also open the gateways to receiving subtle guidance on your life purpose. I'm not talking about some lightning bolt moment where you have complete clarity about why you were born—though anything is possible! But mostly, the guidance you receive during meditation will be small clues and feelings that shed light on solutions to your everyday problems, providing clarity and inspiration for taking aligned action with a focus on what really matters.

This clarity and insight help you move through your day more intentionally. Everything you do throughout your day is at the expense of doing something else. Making meditation a priority greatly helps you gain clarity in your life, so you are utilizing your time and energy to support the highest version of you and not just address the latest distractions.

The value of having clarity about my path showed up while I was writing this book and an opportunity to use new technology to benefit my podcast came up. Although this technology could have helped me create new and different content, learning how to use it and putting it into practice would have taken precious hours away from writing this book, which felt like the stronger imperative at that time. As tempting as it was to increase the visibility of my podcast, I knew deep within me that I needed to focus on writing this book. Diverting my attention from writing to learning and utilizing this new tool would have been a huge distraction that would have taken me out of alignment with what my Higher Self was calling me to do at the time.

There is a concept called slowing down to speed up. When it feels like life is going a million miles a minute, we are most likely not acting from a place of intention. Instead, we are simply responding to life, keeping many balls in the air, dividing our attention, and diffusing our energy. We may feel we are blasting through what needs to be done but not doing anything very well—keeping up, but at a cost. When we slow down, take stock, and become intentional, we can more easily discern what's actually pressing, what can wait, and what doesn't need to be done after all. We gain more control of our time and our lives because we are not at the mercy of the barrage of everything all at once. We develop present moment awareness, and what doesn't matter right now falls away.

Different Strokes for Different Folks

There are many, many meditation methods and techniques that target different results. Meditation can help us focus, feel calmer, overcome stress or pain, be more compassionate or forgiving, process trauma, and so much more. A common component of any meditation is quieting the mind and focusing attention to offset the tugs of distraction. If you are new to meditation, a good place to start quieting your mind is focusing attention on your breath. Focusing on the breath connects us to our bodies and the present moment, which we will explore more deeply later in this chapter. Once connected to the present moment, we can deepen our meditation by bringing our focus to different parts of the body to relax them one at a time. At the end of this chapter, there is a simple meditation practice you can try right now.

As you get more familiar and skilled with focusing your attention during meditation, you can add more elements to your experience. Another common but more advanced meditation technique is using your focus to visualize a specific scene or scenario in which to immerse yourself. Unlike the wandering, unfocused mind of daydreaming, visualization uses focus and imagination to construct a specific experience. You may visualize yourself happily at work in a dream job, totally relaxed in a lush, tranquil natural setting, or that a team of tiny soldiers is coursing through your veins fighting off an infection. These are just some examples of using focus during meditation to create an intentional experience. Be creative. Use your imagination and intuition to tune into the visualizations most beneficial to your life circumstances and spiritual growth.

Realizing Meditation Benefits in the Wild

Building your ability to focus is also enormously helpful outside of meditation. Focusing helps you get the important things done and feel connected to what you are doing, leading to a greater sense of fulfillment. Whatever you are doing throughout your day, give it your focus. If you are writing, write. Put your devices down and set them on Do Not Disturb. If you feel the urge to check your email, social media, or the news, don't indulge it. If you realize you've mindlessly toggled to something else, refocus on your writing. If you are eating dinner with your family, be there with them. Put your phone away; hear them when they ask you questions. Talk to them. If you have teenagers who engage in conversation with you, tell me your secret. If you're cooking, be present with the activity. Bless the food and thank it for its nourishment.

A daily meditation practice is foundational to shifting into a greater connection with your Higher Self. Unplugging from the physical realm and tuning into the invisible aspects of yourself is a gift. Your meditation practice doesn't have to be fancy or overcomplicated. In my own journey, I really benefitted from a teacher and a specific method, and those components made the difference between me dabbling in meditation and having a consistent practice that truly helped me. If you feel that call for a deeper dive, follow your intuition to explore opportunities for connecting with the practice, group, or teacher that is right for you.

ASSERT YOUR INTENTION

You can use your meditation time to be clear with yourself and your Divine guides about your desire to befriend your Higher Self. Open the door to higher consciousness by directly asking for guidance and connection.

My first step to spiritual awakening was inwardly talking to God one day on my walk home from dropping my kids at school. Although I don't have strong religious roots, I adopted an informal practice of sporadically talking to God at different stages of my life. I understood God in the traditional sense of an all-powerful, loving, if not finicky, man in the sky. I can't remember precisely what I said to God on that morning walk, but it was a heartfelt plea to send me some direction as I was coping with the myriad crises of death and life-threatening illnesses and accidents befalling my family all at once.

Considering his already full plate, I wasn't confident that my request would warrant God's action. Rather than really feeling I had the power to effect change with my prayer, I approached the plea more in the spirit of *what do I have to lose?* However, on reflection, I realized that shortly after my plea, I was guided to a meditation master and an organization that was actively teaching his methods, which became a major catalyst for a huge inner transformation.

So, a great first step in establishing your connection to higher consciousness might be simply setting an intention to do so and asking for assistance. Have an inner dialog with God or your Higher Self about how you want to reveal and connect to the hidden aspects of your being. Have this inward discussion with certainty and confidence. Know that you deserve this connection as your birthright and be certain that your Higher Self is waiting for you to request it. It desires this connection very much, but as you are living a human existence, which includes free will, the initiation must come from you. Your request is strengthened with confidence and certainty, such that your Higher Self's response will be unmistakable. Surprisingly, the response is often clearer in hindsight than as it unfolds in front of us.

SOUND HACK

Sound is a powerful and rather sneaky way to connect with your Higher Self through vibrational frequency. Everything is energy, which means everything has a vibration frequency, including our body, mind, and soul. Sound is pure energy and vibration that can quickly resonate or harmonize your human frequency with the frequency of your Higher Self, creating an energetic connection.

Chakras are energy centers within the human body that operate at different vibrational frequencies and can help us connect to our Higher Self through vibrational resonance. There are seven major chakras, starting at the base of the spine and going up to the top of the head. The chakra points have no physicality, but the energy from each chakra governs certain parts of the body, organs, endocrine glands, emotions, and spiritual aspects. Chakras are very multifaceted, relating to many areas of life.

With the help of our chakra centers, sound affects us on energetic levels. Different sound frequencies affect us differently depending on our resonance with the harmonics. An easy way to understand this is to think about how sounds and music in a film guide us on an emotional journey that significantly enhances our experience. We are taken deeper into a movie's drama by well-used musical accompaniment to suspenseful, romantic, thrilling, sad, or celebratory scenes. Casinos and arcade games also use specific sounds at certain pitches and volumes to attract our attention and draw us in. The alerts on our phones and other devices have been carefully crafted to induce specific responses within us, immediately capturing our attention.

Solfeggio Tones

We can choose to listen to sounds such as Solfeggio tones at specific Hertz (Hz) frequencies to stimulate certain aspects of our being. Solfeggio tones are ancient tones blended harmoniously at specific frequencies for a certain outcome. Solfeggio tones also resonate with the vibrational frequencies of each chakra to enhance healing or amplify the energy associated with each chakra. As we listen to the Solfeggio tone, the chakra responds by matching its vibration with the sound waves. Here are the frequencies of recommended Solfeggio tones for each chakra:

- Root 396 Hz

- Sacral 417 Hz

- Solar Plexus 528 Hz

- Heart 639 Hz

- Throat 741 Hz

- Third Eye 852 Hz

- Crown 963 Hz

As we experience life, the chakras can come out of balance and need repair. These imbalances can lead to feeling dis-ease, being out of harmony in our health, relationships, career, purpose, finances, or any other area of life. Chakras can come out of balance when dealing with any number of stressors, illnesses, traumas, toxins, environmental factors, emotions, and so on. Using Solfeggio tones at specific frequencies brings the chakra back into harmony.

You can easily find Solfeggio tones on YouTube or your favorite music streaming service. Search for the frequency number of the chakra energy you are working with, then scroll through the descriptions provided about the purpose of each particular tone to see what you are drawn to.

If you are the type of person who regularly has music on while working or going about your day, imagine the impact on your sense of calm and inner peace if you were to switch from listening to pop music to Solfeggio tones. This simple change can have a palpable impact of shifting you into sustained states of inner peace with little effort.

An effective way to amplify your connection with your Higher Self is to listen to Solfeggio tones that resonate with the third eye and crown chakras or activate the pineal gland. These frequencies will assist you in arousing the higher chakra centers, increasing your resonance with the higher-frequency energies of your Higher Self.

I have had experience with spiritual lineages that focus on the third eye at the expense of interacting at all with the other chakras, including the crown, strangely enough. I have found that approach to be incomplete, to say the least. Overemphasis on your higher chakras does not nurture a balanced inner environment and dismisses very important human aspects of your being. Balance between your physical, emotional, mental, and spiritual bodies is optimal. You are a spiritual being here on Earth, deliberately inhabiting a human body for your soul's development. The lower chakras are linked to the physical, Earthly part of your existence. While you don't want the lower chakras overpowering your spiritual side—higher chakras—neglecting them entirely creates disharmony in the other direction.

You can use Solfeggio or other sounds in or out of meditation:

- To use the sounds during meditation, let your thoughts settle and bring your awareness to the sounds. Breathe slowly and feel the breath low in your torso, as though you are filling your hips. Become aware of the part of the body where the chakra of focus is. If you are playing 396 Hz to work with your root chakra, keep your awareness around the base of your spine. Imagine or feel the sounds vibrating the root. Feel that your root chakra is harmonizing and balancing as the sounds are being absorbed into that energy center. Imagine or feel that the chakra is radiating its harmonized frequency from its center outward.

- Outside of meditation, you can have the sounds on in the background while cooking, working, driving, or any other time it's safe and appropriate. Know that even if you are not keeping your conscious awareness directed at the sounds, they are working with your energy. Just as your skin absorbs sunlight without thinking about it, resulting in your skin pigmentation becoming darker or redder, your energy fields absorb frequency even if you are not concentrating on the sound. Be mindful that the tones make some people feel tired. If that is your experience, don't listen to them while you drive.

PROCESSING TRAUMAS

Emotional trauma holds lower-vibration energy patterns in our bodies, which obstructs the flow of higher-frequency energy needed for connecting with higher consciousness. Healing emotional traumas helps to clear out these stagnant energy patterns, opening us to a greater flow of higher-frequency energy. So often, when we have been through physical or emotional trauma, we are ready to get on the other side of it as quickly as possible. This is natural, as we want to avoid pain. We don't want to dwell on what we've been through because of the pain, discomfort, or shame, or we may fear it so much that we don't feel strong enough to bear the memory. We keep the trauma hidden away as a self-protection mechanism, hoping that if we don't look at it, it won't hurt us again.

Unfortunately, not acknowledging the trauma doesn't make it go away. Instead, it becomes buried within our energy fields and tries to get our attention in other ways, like manifesting as emotional triggers, physical disease, injury, or mental disorders. Unhealed trauma creates vulnerability in the energy fields and chakras where the unhealed energy is buried, making us more prone to experiencing manifest symptoms of imbalanced energy. The more we ignore the painful thoughts and feelings of imbalance, the more pronounced these physical, emotional, or mental symptoms become.

Weakened Energy Points

We can easily see this idea expressed in the physical body when we experience a repeated injury. I was a gymnast as a child and suffered a bad ankle sprain from doing a back handspring when I was eight years old. The swelling was so bad that it hid my ankle and required a wrap that went from my calf to my toes. For the first few days, I could only hobble, causing quite a holdup in the lunch line at school. Being a bit of a glutton for attention, although the injury was quite painful, I initially kind of loved that something different and exciting had happened to me.

Still, it didn't take long for the interest and sympathy from others to wear off, and I was ready to be healed. I followed the doctor's orders and stopped gymnastics for the recommended length of time but resumed the second I was cleared. I expected my ankle to serve me in the same manner it had before the injury and didn't adjust my activities to compensate for any residual weakness or loose tendons. I subsequently kept spraining that same ankle over and over again. Although I never injured it to the same degree, it was exceptionally prone to re-injury. My haste to get back to gymnastics resulted in the ankle being weak and vulnerable for years. Because I made no adjustments for the lost strength and loosened ligaments around my ankle, the physical, emotional, and energetic trauma wasn't fully resolved and continued to manifest as new injuries in the same place.

Decades later, on the day before my 40th birthday, I fractured my foot running in a race. I babied that fracture as best I could until I really felt it was healed. I wore a walking boot and used crutches as needed, accepted the assistance at the airport to ride in one of those carts that beeps at everyone to get out of the way, kept it elevated and iced, and waited until I'd made a full recovery before running again. I also was conservative when I did start running, building up my mileage slowly. That injury never resurfaced.

Hide N' Seek

With trauma, we must witness our pain in order for it to be processed and released. While some kinds of trauma can be fairly benign, like my ankle injury, others can be accompanied by downright terrifying, debilitating circumstances that make us feel completely powerless and fragile. Allowing ourselves to go back to those events in order to face them can be exceptionally difficult, and it feels much safer ignoring them and leaving them in the past. However, unless we process all the levels of healing needed, the trauma doesn't leave us; it hides within us, shaping our experiences behind the scenes in secret ways.

In one of those mysterious multidimensional experiences I mentioned at the start of this chapter, I received a profound lesson related to the idea of the many places where trauma may hide. In my mind's eye, I saw a human body lying horizontally, sliced lengthwise into layers. These layers were stacked together to make a complete human shape. It was akin to thinly slicing a potato and then reassembling it: from a distance, it still looks like a potato, but up close, you can see it's comprised of individual layers.

In this vision, I understood that the layers I was seeing represent everything that makes up the person across time, including everything they have accomplished, witnessed, and experienced throughout this life, as well as all past and future lives. I could see that we store information all through our bodies, not just in our brains. As I received this lesson, my attention was directed to a part of my right arm, where images of my dad and a wolf appeared simultaneously. This showed me that I energetically store both *Dad* and *wolf* in that area of my body.

There appeared to be a link between my dad and a wolf since they showed up together in the same place on my arm. Perhaps my consciousness links them because wolves are hierarchical pack animals, and my dad is naturally a patriarchal figure in my life. Or perhaps some level of my consciousness knows my dad has a wolf spirit animal guide. When I research the spirit totem of the wolf, I see mirrors of my dad's personality in the descriptions: he has a network of loyal friends, prefers diplomacy to open hostility, doesn't like to disturb social order, and more. I didn't know anything about the wolf animal totem prior to that experience, so I wouldn't have picked that specific link to my dad through my human understanding.

Unprocessed Past Life Trauma

Next in this multidimensional experience, I became aware of my friend, Emma, whom I knew to have an imbalance in her throat chakra. During psychic readings and energy healing sessions, she was often told that her throat chakra was out of balance, and I had made this same observation while doing healing work on her. In my vision, Emma was in a big manor house in Great Britain sometime around the 1400s. Although I know her to have a very slim frame, in my vision, she was taller and quite plump. She had on a white bonnet with the straps untied and was working in a big kitchen either on the main floor or a level below. She was going into the *larder*, which I only vaguely knew to be a food storage area but clearly described her whereabouts in my vision. I saw that, unbeknownst to her, someone else was heading toward the larder with a butcher knife.

I knew that she had been fatally wounded in the throat in her encounter with the other person. Because Emma's wound had unexpectedly happened at the very end of her life, she died before she could process the trauma. The energy from the trauma stayed hidden within her from one incarnation to the next, waiting to be seen and healed.

While the vision of Emma's demise perfectly illustrated my insight about layers holding information from all our life experiences, I can't be sure if I saw an actual past life or if the images were just symbolic of how we hold trauma across our lives. Interestingly, just a few hours before I had this vision, Emma had asked me why there was a common theme of a throat chakra issue when she saw different healers and psychics. So perhaps that was easily accessible to my subconscious as a frame of reference for this lesson. When I shared the experience with Emma, she was open to the idea that a fatal wound to her throat may be the root cause of the throat chakra imbalance. I encouraged her not to be too attached to the story as much as considering the possibility that the issue stemmed from another incarnation, relieving her from trying to pinpoint causes from her current life. I suggested that some helpful insights might come through dreams or visions that relate to another time and place.

This multidimensional experience helped me understand that our hidden traumas want to be seen so they can be processed and released. They continue to send us messages to reveal their presence until we get the memo and begin to work with them. This is why talk therapy can be so, well, therapeutic. In a safe environment with someone we trust, we can feel and be with the emotions that remembering a painful experience triggers. Being with difficult emotions while we are feeling safe takes the charge out of them, causing them to lose their grip on us. That stored, dense energy that we were hiding away rises to the surface of our conscious awareness. By acknowledging the pain and feeling the emotions, we can process the trauma and release it.

ENERGY HEALING

While modern medicine and talk therapy have many benefits, working at the energetic level can be an effective and faster approach for healing and releasing stuck lower-vibrational energy and patterns. In many cases, releasing traumas energetically doesn't even require going into the story about the underlying experience surrounding the events that may have caused the trauma. Being caught up in the story of a trauma can feel like living it all over again, causing all the physiological, emotional, and mental responses we endured to be triggered again.

Modalities that work on the energetic level allow the tangled, dense, amassed, and disharmonized energy to be worked with directly so it can come back into balance. The more traditional approach to therapy utilizes the mind to work through trauma. Some people get stuck in their minds and have a hard time overcoming their circumstances simply through mental awareness of what is causing their disharmony. Healing modalities that work at the energetic level go beyond the limitations of the mind.

Changing the energetics can cause things to shift at the human level without having to bring up the memory of the event that caused that tangled energy. Even when trauma is being worked through energetically, as it passes through the layers of our energy and consciousness, we might connect with some parts of the story as they are released. We may feel a sense of sadness or anger as that energy is being released or even feel some flulike symptoms. It is not unusual for tears to be released when receiving energy healing, with or without an understanding of what specifically triggered their liberation. If we let the energy of the trauma pass through us without being attached to it, we can release it for good.

There are many types of energetic healing modalities with many gifted practitioners. Reiki, Energy Editing, hypnosis, neurolinguistic programming, Quantum Healing Hypnosis Technique, Emotional Freedom Technique, Tapping, and energy medicine are just some of the modalities available for energy healing. Many people, including myself, have adapted a learned modality into their own expression of energetic healing, which is organic, innate, and powerful, even if they don't have a name or formula for it. If you want to find an energy practitioner and have no idea where to begin your search, have a look through the episodes of my *Soul Elevation* podcast. I have interviewed many healers on the podcast, and a great starting point is listening to a few of them to see if you resonate with their presence. Many energy workers can work at a distance, so you are not limited by the practitioners who are physically near you unless you prefer to work in person.

Energy Exercises

Whether or not you seek a qualified energy practitioner for alignment and healing, you can maintain healthy and balanced energy on your own. You can incorporate practices like yoga, qi gong, and tai chi into your daily routine. These low-impact exercises are gentle on the body yet highly effective in clearing and harmonizing your energy flow.

Donna Eden is a pioneer in modern energy medicine, and she offers a daily energy routine that is quick and effective in moving energy harmoniously using a combination of tapping, crossing the midline, and tracing the meridians.[5] As mentioned previously, problems that manifest physically, such as illness, disease, and emotional issues, have energetic origins and are manifestations of energetic densities, gaps, and other disharmonies. That means the energy disruption in your system happens *before* the physical manifestation. Donna's energy routine is a series of movements that work directly with your energy system to keep things sealed up and in working order to resolve energy disruptions before they manifest into bigger issues. Her daily energy routine is available on YouTube for regular use to keep your systems running effectively.[6]

BREATHWORK

A sometimes overlooked but simple way to release lower-vibrational energy that may be obstructing our connection with higher consciousness is doing breathwork to improve the flow of energy in our bodies. Considering that illness and accidents follow energetic imbalance, regularly practicing breathwork to strengthen your energy naturally benefits your physical, emotional, and mental fields. At a physiological level, certain breath exercises impact the pH of your blood, helping to make the inner environment of your body more alkaline. Disease requires an acidic inner state and cannot take root when your system is alkaline. Beyond the physical, the breath is well regarded for bringing energy to the nervous system, not only strengthening the energy field but also clearing dense, stagnant energy that is associated with a lower vibration.

There are many breathwork practices, and I encourage you to explore different ones to see what resonates with you. I do breathwork at least once a day. I alternate between several types of breathwork, but my go-to is Wim Hof's method.

Wim Hof, aka *The Iceman*, is a Dutch extreme athlete who has broken a number of records related to cold exposure. He climbed Mount Kilimanjaro in shorts, ran a half marathon barefoot above the Arctic Circle, and was covered with ice cubes for nearly two hours. He has done groundbreaking work to show scientifically how the autonomic nervous system is related to the innate immune response and that it can be consciously and intentionally influenced.

Wim's powerful breathwork method helps you gain access to energy that is trapped in your body. He has many resources to make it easy to learn his methods, which include breathwork, cold therapy, and meditation.[7]

Let's Get Physical

In the first few days of doing Wim's breathing technique, a specific point on my thigh would start vibrating vigorously while doing the breathwork. Then, after a few days, the vibrations stopped. It seemed the quivering vibration was caused by trapped energy in that part of my body that needed to be released. I considered that this may be associated with the energetic remnants of stings I incurred in that area during my beekeeping days. The trapped energy was subtle enough that it had not yet manifested into an injury, rash, or pain. I was able to access the stagnant energy through the breathwork, causing the vibration that activated the energy for release.

So Emotional

Intensive breathwork can also cause an array of emotional responses. During the same time that I was having my vibrating leg experience, I also noticed a sense of anxiety and mild panic during the breathing exercises. Looking back, I concluded that I may have been breathing into some dense energies that were giving me a sense of being trapped on some level. Like the vibrations in my thigh, the emotional response eventually dissolved once I got used to the breathwork.

A much more pronounced emotional response occurred at a retreat I led. We engaged in an intense and amazing hour-long breathwork session that left nearly everyone sobbing. Some had visions featuring departed loved ones that moved them to tears, and others had purely energetic releases with no insights as to their emotional response.

Who's Bad

Breathwork can induce some discomfort physically or emotionally, particularly when you are new to it. Staying neutral and not labeling discomfort as bad will help to move you through the experience. Reserve judgment and simply be curious about how your body and emotions respond to set the stage for transformation. Remember that growth happens just beyond our comfort zone.

Keeping our energy systems aligned through practices such as tai chi, qi gong, yoga, breathwork, or having a trusted practitioner work with our energy through Reiki or other modalities allows us to build the framework to receive and hold more energy from our Higher Self. We are energetic beings, and if our energy systems are cloudy, weak, full of densities and obstructions, or otherwise in need of repair, we are not only vulnerable to health issues but also not robust enough to hold the higher frequencies that come from communication with our Higher Self.

It's Only Natural

The natural world is the perfect setting to get in touch with your Higher Self. Nature helps us shed the buildup of harmful energies that we accumulate throughout our modern lives. Being out in the fresh air, on the land, amidst plants and trees really helps us shift from the demands and stresses of modern life to our natural state of inner peace.

Research has shown that the very act of being with trees calms our nervous system.[8] A popular practice called forest bathing began in Japan as a way to restore energetic balance simply by being in a wooded area and allowing yourself to be cleansed by the natural energy byproduct of trees.

Earthing or grounding is another great practice for connecting with nature. This can be done simply by standing in grass with bare feet, touching the earth with your bare hands, or hugging a tree. Connecting directly with the earth or a tree is especially beneficial for balancing the effects of EMF radiation that we are exposed to throughout the day by modern electronics, which causes a buildup of positive ions in our bodies. Natural environments are abundant with negatively charged ions that help to counteract the imbalance of positive ions and return us to a balanced state.

Earthing also connects us directly to the electromagnetic field of the Earth, which benefits and regulates our own electromagnetic field through an electron exchange between our body and Earth. Free radicals in our bodies are neutralized by these electrons from Earth. Other benefits from grounding and just being in nature generally are reducing inflammation, improving circulation, lifting your spirits, and stabilizing cortisol levels, which helps with sleep and stress.

Chakra Balancing

Beyond the physical, connecting with nature helps us to experience ourselves as part of a bigger ecosystem. Nature is organically expansive, and the human body has evolved lockstep with it to have an optimized human experience on Earth. Removing ourselves from nature to the degree that most of us have in our modern world has separated us from this imperative relationship with the natural world. By connecting more with the natural world, we balance and restore the energies of our chakra system. Our lower chakras, in particular, are connected to nature, and being in nature automatically connects us to the energy in the associated chakra.

The root chakra at the base of the spine is connected to solid, earthy energy. Through the element of water, we connect to the sacral chakra, which is below the belly button, in the general area of the sex organs. Fire connects us to the solar plexus at the top of the abdomen, just below where the ribcage comes together. The wind and air connect us to our heart chakra at the center of the chest. We automatically stimulate and help to balance out these chakras when we interact with the various aspects of nature.

Consciousness flows through all of nature. As we become more aligned with our higher levels of consciousness, we more easily attune ourselves to the consciousness of the trees, plants, minerals, water, fire, and air in a symbiotic, mutually beneficial way. We see that all these natural elements are a part of one another. They are a part of us, and we are a part of them.

RETREATING

The quickest and most powerful way I have experienced strengthening my Higher Self connection is on a spiritual retreat. A retreat is different from a vacation. In addition to unplugging from the rest of your life as you do on vacation, you are also diving deeply into your psyche, stepping back to consider your life from a broader perspective, and taking time to reassess what is important to you, who you want to become, and if you are heading in the right direction to get there.

For the most part, we live life day-to-day, caught in the daily demands and challenges. We are tangled in the mire of everyday life, and separating from the moment-to-moment demands to assess if we are tracking in the direction of the highest version of ourselves is difficult. We navigate life through the lens of programming and habitual patterns that keep us firmly rooted in our current phase of development. Going on a retreat helps to break us out of those patterns so we can give ourselves the kick we need to get into the next phase of expansion.

During a retreat, you spend a concentrated amount of uninterrupted time nurturing your spiritual connection, allowing space for you to experience great expansions and breakthroughs. What may take you years to gain insight into and enlightenment about against the backdrop of hectic, modern-day living can come to you in a flash in the right environment.

Expanding My Balloon

A few years ago, I had four different retreat-type opportunities in the course of about six weeks, resulting in the biggest metaphysical experience I had had to date. First, I spent a long weekend at the Omega Institute in New York. The center was located in a beautiful spot in nature, and there were daily meditations and wonderful, whole-food meals. I went on my own to immerse myself in the topic of energy medicine and see speakers like Dr. Sue Morter and Donna Eden.

A couple of weeks later, we took a short family vacation to Arizona and spent half a day in Sedona. Sedona is a vortex site with unusual, heightened energies throughout the land. We took a spiritual vortex tour to experience particularly potent spots in the area. The tour was very activating for me. Most importantly, I met my mentor and friend, Michael, for the first time. After that, I had my first Reiki training weekend, which included beautiful ceremonial activations. I met wonderful people and had a powerful time. Shortly afterward, I joined a local yoga retreat focused on energy work led by Dr. Sue Morter. People had flown in from all over the country and beyond, but it happened to be less than 10 minutes from my house.

Each of these retreat experiences was different, and each one expanded my consciousness more and more, with many energetic shifts in a short period of time. Looking back on that period of time, I can see the grand, intelligent design in spending a few days in great expansion, then returning to daily life to integrate the shifts in consciousness and allow the new energies to anchor in and normalize before setting out again for another immersive expansion. I like the metaphor of blowing up a balloon to describe the experience. First, you blow as much breath as you can into the balloon to fill it with air, expanding it until you need to catch your breath. Then, you pinch the opening to steady the expansion while inhaling to fill your lungs for the next blow and repeat this until the balloon is fully expanded. Fill, pause, recharge, and fill again.

Culmination of the Expansion

My first ever multidimensional experience happened on the first night at the yoga retreat. I was riding a high vibration of excitement in anticipation of the coming days, and it was taking a while to fall asleep. Suddenly, behind my closed eyes, I saw flashes of colored lights with different geometric shapes. It was incredibly beautiful and completely unexpected! I had no idea what I was seeing, but I knew it was a gift.

The next day I received a text from Michael, the guide on my Sedona vortex tour, that said he felt he was supposed to connect with me. I hardly knew Michael then, so getting any text from him was unusual, much less one that hinted at intuiting my mystical experience. Given the serendipitous timing, I decided to tell him about my experience with the flashes of light and geometric shapes in case he had any insights, given I didn't know anything about multidimensionality and hardly had words for what had happened. Micheal suggested that the experience was an activation to wake up a part of my consciousness that had been dormant or asleep. He also felt that his impetus to contact me in conjunction with my experience signaled his guiding role in what would become a rapid awakening for me.

SILENCE SPEAKS

Silence is fundamental to connecting to your Higher Self. Having a string of days offline and in complete silence takes you into a deep level of stillness and peace. Considering I am still raising my children, who rely on my presence and interaction, disconnecting for long periods of silent time and going deep into silence is a luxury I don't experience often. However, I improvise by developing a regular practice of going offline for a few hours of uninterrupted time. Especially with family and work demands, it requires a concerted effort to put aside any everyday pressures and carve out time to be completely alone. It's imperative to block out time on the calendar and hold it sacred, to be interrupted only in the most urgent circumstances.

What you do with your silent time can vary as long as it brings you to a place of inner peace and self-reflection. Resist any self-pressure to *make good use* of the time offline by attending to daily tasks, like laundry. Put your phone away; don't engage with your email or social media. Take a break entirely from screens and get a respite from blue light and flat, two-dimensional interactions. The point is not *just* to be silent but to put yourself into a sacred space through activities that lift your vibration and take you out of your routine. Meditating, doing yoga or tai chi, journaling, being in nature, chanting or toning, and just being are all excellent ways to make the most of this sacred time. Fasting or eating lightly with vibrant, fresh food enhances the experience by keeping your energy light and focused on the inner planes.

I enjoy carving out a few hours for my silent time when my kids are at school. Life goes on around me, and I am available when they get home from school to continue with the usual family routine. But through this block of silent time, I am able to shed the buildup of modern life and shift into a higher vibration.

JOURNALING

Journaling is another great practice for connecting to your Higher Self. It is a powerful way to get into a creative flow and rhythm. Through writing, we ground higher thoughts, ideas, and feelings into the physical plane. We take these thoughts and inspirations, which are floating around us like etheric puffs of cotton on the wind, grab them and pull them down into our experience where they can be seen and reflected upon.

Journaling is done for yourself to organize your thoughts and feelings and record your experiences. You aren't submitting it to anyone else, so relax any discomfort you may feel about your grammar, spelling, or any other literary concepts that are rusty since the time of submitting essays in English class. Your journal is a way for you to communicate with yourself across time or possibly to help you process what you are going through without ever looking at your entry again.

There are many different types of journaling. You can buy journals that contain prompts to prime your pump of inspiration to help you get started, especially if you are new to writing down your thoughts. Personally, I prefer to find a pretty, blank journal that I use for capturing my thoughts on certain topics that I have found to be particularly productive for personal reflection and connecting with higher consciousness. The following journaling topics are suggestions for writing prompts that will strengthen your connection to these higher vibrational aspects of your consciousness.

Gratitude

A powerful focus for journaling is gratitude. The secret behind gratitude journaling is that we naturally draw into our lives what we focus on. When we focus on gratitude, we get into the frequency of being thankful. The stronger that frequency is within us, the more we naturally reside in it when we aren't even trying to bring it into our awareness. Simply said, the more grateful we are, the more easily we attract things into our lives for which we are grateful.

Let that sink in. Pause for a moment and really let yourself receive this powerful truth.

The more grateful we are, the more we naturally attract into our life things for which we are grateful.

Another way to think of it: *What we appreciate, appreciates.*

Getting into the feeling of gratitude as much as you can is exceptionally powerful. Take time once or twice a day to think of things in your life for which you are grateful and write them down. With a dedicated, joyful effort, you can experience big shifts from this simple practice.

Dreams

The dream state is a fertile time for connecting to higher states of consciousness. We naturally access other levels of consciousness while sleeping. Our dreams often speak to us in symbols rather than literally. Writing down the dreams while fresh in your mind can help you pick through symbolism later. Taking time to consider what the different elements that show up in a dream mean helps reveal their hidden messages and insights. You may have a dream that features a fireplace, a secret room, a child, and a pocket watch. Upon waking, you may not be able to connect to any symbolism from those elements, but if you jot them down and reflect on them later, you may weave together a meaningful metaphor for your life.

A quick internet search will pull up lots of websites that offer meanings for common symbols that appear during the dream state. So, if you are stuck on what something like a fireplace might represent for you, you can investigate a more universal meaning. If an animal appears in your dream, you can visit an animal totem site to learn what that animal generally represents.

I keep a notebook next to my bed, and if I can remember my dream, I will write it down as soon as I wake up. It is remarkable just how slippery dreams can be. There have been many times that I thought I could wait to write something down because my dream was so real and vivid as I came out of it that it seemed there was no way I'd forget it. But I can hardly remember it in a matter of minutes or even seconds. The veils that blanket our waking minds and shroud our dream memories come on thick and fast. A distraction upon waking can evaporate the memory of a dream from my consciousness in no time.

Often, my dreams are not meaningful to me right away. Sometimes, something referenced in a dream will appear later in the day. By then, my dreams from the night before are usually very foggy, so being able to review what I captured in my journal is helpful. In one of my vivid dreams, my dad gave me a special gift of three semi-circles connected vertically. They were different sizes and different shades of light purple. It was very beautiful and special. In the dream, he said it was made by Frank Lloyd Wright. Two days later, I was interviewing someone on my podcast who told a story about a house designed by Frank Lloyd Wright's son. While I know who Frank Lloyd Wright is, he doesn't come up very often in my life. So, hearing his name in a vivid dream and a podcast interview two days later definitely caught my attention. I did not draw any particular conclusion from this convergence, but I was left with an appreciation of how we may see or access aspects of a future experience in the dream state.

Another interesting phenomenon related to dream journaling is reviewing dreams from the past with an eye to how they may have messages or offer something relevant to the current moment. Reading a journal entry from months ago that has relevance to the present is thrilling. You can see a divine masterpiece at work throughout the fabric of time as your past dream state points to your present. You can flip through your journal at random, and it feels like your Higher Self is reaching through time to touch your heart.

Divine Connections

Wisdom and inspiration are often received during a meditative state. Journaling about these insights helps you track your progression toward higher levels of awareness and consciousness, assisting you in revealing a bigger-picture perspective about your life experiences. Over time, you may notice patterns that reveal a particular area of focus for your spiritual awakening. The more you meditate, the more likely you will experience multidimensional phenomena, such as seeing lights or colors, feeling benevolent presences, hearing sounds, feeling sensations, noticing smells, or having a new sense of knowing. Writing down these experiences as your own witness to this evolution is very helpful and encouraging as a continued reminder of your expanding abilities to connect with the Divine, be it your Higher Self or other aspects of higher consciousness.

It's very natural to feel great progress in meditations for a period and then enter into a dry spell where you aren't feeling or perceiving much when you drop into a meditative state. In those times, it may be difficult to remember the powerful ways you had previously perceived contact from your Higher Self. You can easily convince yourself that you are unable to connect with your Higher Self or that meditation is a waste of your time. These self-sabotaging thoughts couldn't be further from the truth! Take comfort in knowing that everyone goes through these phases and stages and use your meditation journal to help you remember your experiences of connecting with divinity.

Top 10 List

Michael suggested that I have an ongoing Top 10 Peak Experiences list to easily access the frequency of divine connection and higher consciousness encounters and benefit from them at any time, and I recommend that you implement this in your life, too. Take time to thoughtfully develop a list of the top ten times you have felt most connected to your Higher Self, Source, or some other aspect of higher consciousness that absolutely lit you up that you want to hold in your heart forever. Jot down every amazing experience you can think of, then whittle the list down to ten based on how expansive and uplifted they make you feel. As the memories come to you, try to get into the feeling or vibration of each experience. Take your time to create your Top 10 list. The point is not just to recount what happened but to really get your energy, brain, heart, and cells back into that place. You are using the quantum field to reach back through time so you can be in that vibe again. Emotions are an important gateway to get back into the experience, so connecting with how the experience made you *feel* is critical.

Once your list is created, refer to it regularly. Give yourself the time and space to reflect on each experience within your list, allowing the frequency of the experience to move through you. As you spend more time with your list, you can become proficient in using it to raise your vibration because it creates a bridge from where you are at any given time to those peak experience times; your being responds as though that peak experience is happening now. This can be an awesome tool to use when you feel the shadows of negative energy penetrating your thoughts and making you forget the incredible embodiment of divine light that you truly are. Our brains have a hard time discerning between what is real, imagined, or remembered. Showering yourself in the energy of a divine connection signals to the brain that this is your reality, and the brain responds by shifting your experience of your inner and outer world.

LEST WE FORGET

If you notice an inner voice that sounds an awful lot like you whispering that your meditation time isn't worth it, your time would be better spent doing something other than sitting around in meditation, or that you are small and ineffectual, whip out your divine connections journal and soak in those high-vibe experiences. Armed with the evidential truth of Who You Are, that shadow will lose its voice. *Nice try, sneaky voice—not today!*

I did a podcast interview with Jamie Butler, a gifted psychic medium, channeler, Reiki master, and spiritual teacher.[9] She talked about the necessity of reminding ourselves about our divine experiences. When initiating someone into Reiki, she keeps checking in with them to help them integrate new feelings and experiences that may arise from connecting with higher-frequency energy so it may have a more sustained or lasting impact. Her Reiki students may feel in the moment that they will never forget such an impactful experience or see life in the same way. Inevitably, they return to their daily lives, resuming their routines, habits, and thoughts, and their Reiki initiation experiences fade into the background. They might even begin to doubt their divine experience as everyday life closes in around them. Jamie continually works with her students to help deepen their experiences of the higher frequencies, and recording your high-frequency experiences in a journal serves that same purpose.

Other special moments of divine connection that you may want to write about in your journal are synchronicities you experience, soul connections you have made, high-frequency discussions you've had, or wisdom you've received from books or courses that really resonated with you, nurturing your soul. Journaling these details can help illuminate the magic happening in your life as you deepen your connection with your Higher Self. Writing about these experiences solidifies them in your conscious mind and keeps them from quickly fading into the background of mundanity.

SLEEP STATE

During sleep, we move through and access different levels of consciousness, sometimes connecting us with higher consciousness or our Higher Self. The subconscious mind is able to dress up some of these experiences as dreams, leaving traces of images that we may remember on waking. But the vast majority of our sleep time experience is inaccessible once awake. The little-self mind doesn't carry the memory from the sleep state into waking consciousness.

However, we can gain some ability to direct the sleep state through intention by stating what we desire our consciousness to focus on while we are sleeping. Before engaging in sleep-time work, it's extremely important to establish a protective energy field around our body. Whenever we work to expand our consciousness, intentionally or unintentionally, we open up our energy fields, exposing vulnerabilities in areas where we are still working through our shadow energies. You might think of these spots of energetic vulnerability as similar to open skin wounds. In the same way that we need a band-aid to keep germs and bacteria from entering our bodies through an open wound, we need a protective shield to keep lower-vibrational entities from entering our energy field. Invoking protective light and aligning with Source and our Higher Self is like putting on a beautiful cosmic band-aid of protection.

In order to intentionally use my sleep state in the highest way, I utilize this practice before falling asleep:

1. I surround myself with protective light and ask for support and protection while I am sleeping.

2. I invoke the presence of my Divine Team and ask for their presence while I sleep. I ask them to appear in my dreams and assist me in remembering them.

3. I set the intention and make requests to the Universe for my sleep time to be productive. Depending on what is happening in my life at the time, I may make a specific request about what I want to focus on. For example, if someone I know is going through a rough time or has recently died, I may ask that my consciousness be used to assist them energetically in the most effective way.

I highly recommend this practice because, in the years that I have taken these steps before falling asleep, I have greatly improved my ability to remember my dreams, very rarely experience nightmares, and have had many profound dreams that feel like interactions with the spiritual realm. Even if you don't see immediate results, trust that your continued dedication will build up to more profound experiences. Sleep time is so fertile and a huge portion of our lives. Invite it to be a time to further your development, trusting that with the intention of strengthening your connection to Source and your Higher Self, you will continue to progress toward your expansion and evolution.

Dream Screen

In my nighttime multidimensional experiences, I can catch myself as I fall asleep and either wake up or continue into sleep. As I drift into sleep, I start to notice stories unfolding. Forms begin to morph out of the geometries, light, and underlying structure of the multidimensional experience. From these recurring experiences, I have learned that, on some level, dreams are our human mind's interpretation of the activities of our higher consciousness that we are unaware of as we sleep. In essence, dreams *humanize* our non-human experiences in the sleep state.

All of the practices suggested in this chapter will assist you in shifting your reality into one infused with the presence of your Higher Self. Small changes accumulate and bear fruit in a gentle way that doesn't require an abrupt about-face that can cause us and those who love us to be smacked with a suddenly unfamiliar version of ourselves. While we might wish for a quick and dramatic transformation into a higher version of ourselves, the price can be losing our grip on this shared human reality. Being purposeful and effective in life is difficult if we are questioning our sanity. Trust that as you adjust your life to align with your Higher Self more and more, you will begin to experience the flow of divinity.

These types of changes invite a higher vibration into our lives. Often, we want the proof before we set the stage for divinity to enter.

We might think, "If I'm going to make these changes, I want to know it's going to get me something special."

In truth, we need to make the changes to align ourselves to higher-frequency energies and consciousness so the proof can come in. We must clear out and release the energetic gunk to make space for these higher-frequency expressions and experiences. If we continue living the way we always have, we will keep experiencing the same results. By actively raising our frequency through actions like those in this chapter, we show the Universe the uplifted life we want to create, and the Universe will respond in kind.

TRANSFORMATION OF FREE WILL

As great sages have observed, you cannot plant a seed and then continuously dig it up to check its progress. Plant your seeds to connect to your Higher Self, then nurture and water them faithfully with your continued practices. Over time, you will begin to see them germinate and reach ever toward the light.

An interesting phenomenon often begins as the seeds of awakening grow roots, and the seedling starts to mature—you begin to build momentum. At a certain point, your free will transforms, and it seems there is no longer a choice. You become so aligned with your Higher Self that the highest choice seems the only one. In truth, you are always choosing. Even if the inner guidance is so strong that it feels like the choice has been made for you, you are still choosing to follow it.

Remember the great reveal I shared of a huge soul opportunity on many levels that existed for all involved if I asked a particular person to invest in my book? The highest solution was laid out clearly before me, but I could still choose something emotionally easier in the short term to avoid the discomfort required for the higher path. Becoming aligned with your Higher Self and your divinity allows your life to be in service to the Divine through the actions you take, the words you say, and the way you express yourself.

This chapter contains lots of practical ways to strengthen your connection to your Higher Self. We talked about meditation, sound, asking for connection, healing, working directly with your energy, spending time in nature, taking a spiritual retreat, silence, journaling, and using sleep time. Is there something on that list that you are not currently practicing? Pick one practice that is new to you and develop a habit of it.

If you have not already incorporated meditation into your life, I highly recommend giving it a try. It doesn't need to be complicated.

Here is a simple method for getting started.

1. Close your eyes. Imagine you are surrounded by golden or white light. Take a deep, cleansing inhale through your nose and sigh it out through your mouth. Repeat this two times.

2. Relax your body. Start at the feet and relax each part of the body: feet, lower legs, upper legs, tummy, chest, shoulders, arms, hands, neck, and head.

3. Continue to breathe deeply and slowly in and out of your nose. Keep your attention with the flow of breath. If you get distracted by thoughts, gently acknowledge this, let the thoughts go, and return your focus to your breath.

4. Focus deeper and deeper on the flow of breath. After several breaths, allow yourself to breathe naturally without controlling it. Be inside your body, observing the stillness. Enjoy basking in this stillness for as long as you wish. When you're ready, open your eyes.

CHAPTER 4

A LITTLE HELP FROM YOUR INVISIBLE FRIENDS

On any journey, it's wise to be prepared for what you might encounter. By the very nature of going on an adventure, you are leaving what is familiar and comfortable to experience new terrain, opening yourself to the possibility of seeing unimaginably beautiful vistas, meeting interesting people, and discovering new things. New experiences unfold for your enjoyment as you stretch yourself through your exploration. Because you are stepping into unfamiliar territory, you may encounter some unpleasant surprises during your travels.

While some paths may be lined with bright, fragrant fauna and culminate in a sparkling waterfall, others may be dimly lit with treacherous footing and lead you into a valley when you are looking for a summit.

So it is on a spiritual journey. The unseen realms you are traversing comprise a whole spectrum of energies you may encounter. But rather than passing judgment about these energy frequencies by labeling them good or bad, consider that everything is Source energy expressing itself through an endless gradient of higher and lower frequency energies. Some energy frequencies are full of light and benevolence, desiring your evolution and highest good. Others are low, darker, and oppressive, seeking to manipulate and use your energy for their gain.

Humanity itself exists on a similar spectrum. Some people aim to help you, while others you would prefer not to encounter in a dark alley. Each individual also possesses a spectrum of motivations, perceptions, and agendas at any given time within their own unique personality. Fortunately, you have the powerful tools of prayer and protection at your disposal to create strong spiritual boundaries so you can progress confidently on your path in alignment with frequencies most beneficial to your journey.

THE TENSION FROM NO INTENTION

If you are drawn to reading this book, it's likely your intention is to open yourself to a connection with higher frequency energies and consciousnesses that serve your highest good. Being clear about this intention as you begin your meditation, sleep, or any other activity of traversing consciousness is important because it sets restrictions on the type of energy welcome to engage with you while your energy fields are relaxed and open. Without a clear intention to connect only with ethereal consciousnesses that serve your highest good, you are essentially leaving the door open for attracting unwanted lower-frequency energy beings looking for vulnerable entry points in your energy field.

The power of human intention cannot be overemphasized, including when traversing the unseen realms. You are the commander of your experience. Give your intention the backing of your confidence, knowing that the more you embody your authentic soul nature, the more the Universe must organize Itself according to your intention.

My Formula to Set the Stage for Meditation or Sleep

When engaging in experiences to expand consciousness, my goal is to raise my vibrational frequency and connect to my Higher Self and Divine guides. To ensure my energy field is best aligned to achieve that connection, I am deliberate about the level of the frequency spectrum I wish to access when shifting into other states of consciousness.

In a livestream for my podcast, my guest, Maureen St. Germain, recommended setting an intention to only engage with beings of 100% God light.[10] She explained that if she

118 | Your Authentic Awakening

feels she is receiving communication from beyond the veil, she commands that it is welcome only if it comes from a source of 100% pure God light. If the communication continues, she can trust it is aligned with her decree.

Since my conversation with Maureen, I have followed her advice and taken the time to qualify any subtle energies I perceive by inwardly saying they are welcome if they are aligned with 100% pure God light. Otherwise, they must leave. Sometimes, as I go about my day, I will get a loud tone in my ear or feel my inner ear vibrate, which can be a signal from the spirit realms.

When I notice it, I will say, "I welcome contact with those of 100% pure God light."

If the communication continues, I am confident that what is coming through is for my highest good.

For this reason, I recommend starting every meditation by placing yourself in a protective bubble of golden or white light. Feel or intend that this light is nurturing and supporting you, acting as a filter that allows only aligned energy to be part of the meditation. Nothing else can pass through the filter. It is a formidable bouncer at the door of the consciousness party.

Once you have placed yourself in the bubble of light, continue by setting the intention of who is welcome in that practice. You can think of this as a simple intention, a prayer, an invocation, or a decree. Remember that you are in charge.

You get to say who or what is invited to the party. Empower yourself by owning your command. This is *your* meditation, *your* space, *your* energy fields.

I utilize the following invocation for calling in my guides that I adapted from several sources, including a course offered by Sandra Walter on her website, Ascension Path, to call in my guides.[11]

> *I welcome forth my Higher Self, Christed Self, I AM presence, and Pure Source Consciousness.*
>
> *I invite in my Divine Team: Angels and Archangels, Ascended Masters, and benevolent star family.*
>
> *I invite in only those who are aligned with pure Source, for my highest good. All of those known and unknown who are assisting in my ascension, thank you for your guidance, love, and support.*

Within the invocation, I call in specific guides I feel drawn to in my personal journey. The guides I may call on include Archangels Gabriel, Raphael, Michael, and Zaphkiel, and Ascended Masters Yeshua (Jesus), Babaji, Quan Yin, and Buddha. I may also call on star family, meaning extraterrestrial races I feel particularly connected to, such as the Andromedans, Sirians, Pleiadians, Arcturians, and Mantis beings of light. Because extraterrestrial races vary in levels of evolution, I add the qualifying term *beings of light* to clarify that only those beings working with and for pure Source consciousness, aligned with high-frequency light-love energy, are called forth.

I state this invocation either out loud or silently. The spoken word is more powerful and can help me stay focused throughout the invocation. However, if I gather my focus and stay mindful of my intention while saying it silently, it's just as effective.

You are welcome to use it in whatever capacity you choose. Some or all of it may feel right to you; there may be some parts you wish to adopt and others that don't resonate. Take what you want, leave out what you don't, and feel free to add anything that resonates with you. I often make little adjustments, adding in and taking out as I feel inspired in the moment.

After calling my Divine Team into the meditation, I thank them and bless them for their guidance and protection. I also mention any specific areas I want to work on or amplify through the meditation. These are some of my more frequent areas of focus:

- Strengthening connection with my Higher Self

- Healing physical ailments

- Dissolving disharmonious, harmful, or self-sabotaging thought patterns

- Awakening dormant gifts

- Harmonizing difficulties with others

- Resolving emotional triggers

- Receiving inspiration or solutions to problems

- Raising my vibration

THE DANCE

Meditation can be a beautiful dance between surrender and command. Explore the space between directing your experience through prayer and receiving what is bestowed upon you. Once I have set an intention and completed the invocation, I relax and fully embrace an open and receptive state. Being intentional is not the same as needing to control every aspect of the meditation. Relaxation, acceptance, and allowing are crucial for accessing higher frequencies.

As I move into a deeper state of receptivity, I trust my Higher Self and God to present things to me in divine timing in a beautiful, meaningful, and delightful way. While little human Kara may desire immediate results, there is a delicate masterpiece unfolding before me, the genius of which I can hardly fathom.

Prayer is a way of communicating with the intelligent cosmic force that flows through everything. It has been said that prayer is talking to God, and meditation is listening for the response. While I recommend you begin your meditations by being clear about your intentions and reinforcing your energetic boundaries, you may also want to share your hopes and desires with God, as well as your prayers for the healing and well-being of others. Sometimes, I find it easier to have a more free-flowing inner dialog with God toward the end of my meditation after I've had time to get really relaxed and raise my frequency. Give yourself time and space in the stillness of meditation to listen for a response to your prayers.

Although getting still and quieting your thoughts is the optimal way to listen for a response to your prayers, you don't need to be in meditation to pray effectively. You can commune with God whenever you open yourself to that connection. Don't limit yourself by thinking you can only pray if you are on your meditation cushion. Pray on the go, too —in the car, at the grocery store, brushing your teeth, whenever it comes to mind. Keeping communication going outside of meditation will help you continue to strengthen your connection to the Divine. The more often you tune into your divine union while going about your daily life, the more you will benefit and find inner guidance for navigating your life path.

While I have some guidelines for adding a prayer practice to your meditation and daily life, don't let my suggestions, or any practice for that matter, devolve into rigid prescriptions. If you overthink your prayer, you will miss the feeling aspect. Your feelings and emotions build the energy of the prayer. Just allowing a memorized prayer to spill out of your mouth with no genuine connection weakens its effect.

HIGHEST OUTCOMES

If it seems that your prayer is not answered, remember the wisdom of the myriad mysterious ways our lives unfold in accordance with our highest purpose. Praying for what you desire with the ultimate intention of serving the highest good ensures this alignment, even if the immediate result isn't what you expected.

From our little human perspective, we may think we know the best and highest outcome for problems. If someone we love is sick, we may believe the absolute highest resolution is for them to be cured. However, our limited human understanding lacks the ability to know the divinely devised course of another's soul journey. The lessons they gain from their illness and treatment could be key triggers for setting them on an important path to helping others. Through that experience, they may discover hidden truths within themselves or realize their priorities have been misplaced, leading them to initiate a course correction that they would never have considered if they had been floating along in ease and comfort. Even their death can be a divine orchestration serving the highest purpose for their soul and those they have left behind.

AMP IT UP

Much of my prayer time is during meditation when I am most focused on the wholeness of who I am beyond my human expression. I find that being intensely focused within the stream of connection to my Higher Self significantly amplifies the power of my prayers.

A common mental hurdle can be the feeling that we have to *send* prayers across vast distances to where someone is physically located. If you're in America praying for someone in Asia, you may feel like you don't have enough power or energy for the prayers to make it across all those miles. But prayers happen in the quantum realm, where space is an illusion. Through your focus, intention, and attention, you can lift someone in prayer regardless of where their body is located.

If you feel that you need a little help to overcome this mental hurdle, build up the energy in your heart. Feeling your prayers swim in the energy of the heart increases your prayer power. To do this, close your eyes and take some deep, slow breaths. Bring your awareness into the center of your chest, where the spiritual heart is located. Feel that you are breathing in and out of your heart. Let it be easy; don't overthink it. Simply be aware of the heart area.

As you bring your awareness into the heart, you automatically draw more energy into it. Wherever we direct our thoughts, attention, and awareness is where the energy goes. Tiny units of energy called photons are attracted together wherever you send your awareness. The longer you keep your awareness on one thing, the more energy builds up there. Allow the energy to grow and increase in your heart.

Then imagine you are bringing the person into your healing heart energy. Visualize or imagine infinite streams of high-frequency, golden, or green light radiating from your heart and running around and through it. Visualize these streams of light, releasing anything not serving them and filling them with divine love, light, and peace. See them in their happiest, healthiest state as you hold them in your heart's light. Know that while you are bathing them in this beautiful energy, you are also benefitting from it in a natural and reciprocal way.

A Healer Reveals My Secret

A few months after I began my meditation practice, I had a mysterious experience that shifted my perspective of the effect of prayer on the heart from theoretical to observable. I attended a weekend retreat focused on Paramahansa Yogananda's teachings about opening the heart where I received my first healing session with an energy practitioner. During the session, I received an energy reading of my chakra system, starting with my root chakra and moving up to my crown chakra. For each chakra, I was given insights about my life that were relevant and meaningful, along with suggestions about how to move through my challenges or open myself up to more opportunities.

I will never forget the impact of the insight I was given about my heart chakra. To my surprise, I was told that my heart would open up much more if I prayed before meditating. I was somewhat shocked by this observation because beginning meditation with prayer is fundamental to

Yogananda's teachings, and, indeed, I had not incorporated this into my practice. While it would be logical to assume that all retreat participants following the teachings of Yogananda prayed before meditating, the intuitive insights I received from this energy practitioner were spot on.

While I had embraced many of Yogananda's methods, I had not yet become comfortable with the more esoteric practice of prayer. I was fascinated by the physiological effects of meditation: how calming the breath soothes the mind and nervous system and how focusing on a mantra can deepen concentration. However, I remained unconvinced about the benefit or necessity of prayer.

The profundity of the experience encouraged me to prioritize beginning my meditations with prayer. Initially, my prayer practice was dogmatic, following a prescribed opening prayer taught through that spiritual lineage. Gradually, I felt more of an organic opening and connection to God in my heart through prayer.

What ultimately became the most vital part of my practice was the slowest and most resistant to emerge. Now, my meditation practice is centered on connecting to my Higher Self to open my heart and align with Source. Prayer is a foundational component of that divine connection.

Pumping the Brakes

Consistent prayer communicates with your guides that you welcome their assistance and clarifies the direction for spiritual growth you wish to take. Earth is a free-will zone. We are free to awaken or not. Spiritual evolution cannot be forced upon us. Just as we cannot pry open a flower to force its bloom, your Divine Team will not impose upon or interfere with your free will to awaken your spiritual nature if it is not in divine timing.

In my opening prayer, I communicate my desire to keep going in my spiritual development. But that kind of focused intention can get overwhelming— like being in school 24/7 without a break! Depending on what's happening in your life or your current emotional or mental state, your ability to adapt and integrate life lessons may require adjustments along the way. If things get too intense, you may need to pause your spiritual pursuits, and that is OK!

Just like setting a prayer intention to continue your spiritual expansion and awakening gives a clear "We are a GO!" to your Higher Self and guides, not sending this intention signals your team to pump the brakes and slow down. There is no judgment. It's your free will choice to decide the intensity and pace of your spiritual growth.

Remember the metaphor of the electricity converter and the importance of not getting overloaded or receiving too much too fast. You are having this experience on Earth, not your

Divine Team. While your team has ideas and observations of what it is like for you, they aren't here in the physical realm experiencing your life. Feeling maxed out, tired, stressed, irritable, spacey, disconnected from reality, or lethargic can be signs from your physical, mental, or emotional bodies that you need a pause. Take it.

INTEGRATION STATION

Continuous expansion with no emphasis on integration can cause you to feel confused, off-center, or unable to relate to yourself or others. By integration, I mean allowing yourself time to adapt and get used to changes resulting from increasing your vibrational frequency and expanding your consciousness to incorporate new awareness and energies. Remember the earlier analogy of blowing up a balloon and needing that pause to fill your lungs back up with air? Never underestimate the importance of patience and pausing to integrate each expansion period before filling your balloon with more air.

A helpful analogy about the need for spiritual integration is how our bodies integrate changes in diet. With a crash diet, you put all your attention and energy into losing weight fast at a high cost to your health and nutrition. You might try things you would never choose otherwise, such as eating only cabbage soup for days, replacing food with a pill, or not eating for several days. Although you will likely lose weight, the deprivation drains your body of vitamins, vital nutrients, and hydration. The physical drain can cause your emotions to come undone, putting stress on personal interactions with your family, friends, and colleagues. Aside from health concerns, crash diets are not suited to long-term everyday living, and eventually, the weight comes back when the protocols are stopped.

Comparatively, a more long-term sustainable approach to weight loss that allows you to integrate changes to your diet and lifestyle gradually is a more certain path to success. Focusing on bringing greater health into your life by eating foods rich in vitamins and minerals, eliminating sugars and processed foods, and being mindful of the pace and frequency with which you eat and other patterns around food not related to your hunger response results in the weight loss being more lasting than with a crash diet. Your body will get nourishment for optimal health, and you will be spared the emotional roller coaster ride. With persistence and patience, you will experience healthy weight loss as excess fat, toxins, and accumulated gunk are flushed out.

Similarly, with your spiritual development, you can choose daily practices designed to achieve and sustain higher levels of consciousness by gradually clearing low-frequency thoughts and behaviors that allow for a more consistent connection with higher-frequency energies. However, there are also methods for engaging in a fast, explosive spiritual experience akin to the crash diet. One fairly common method to achieve such immediate and profound shifts of consciousness is the use of psychedelics.

While using psychedelics in a specific and controlled environment with a skilled guide can be a life-changing catalyst for massive change, frequent recreational use can be damaging to physical, mental, and emotional health. Psychedelics can potentially deliver a peak experience where reality is experienced in a completely new way. But with no spiritual framework to anchor the experience to your everyday life, it will not shift you into a higher frequency long term. The highest opportunity for utilizing psychedelics is to experience the mind-expanding wonder they can bring forth and allow that wonder to propel you to make changes that shift your everyday life to a higher frequency. Truly embodying a higher frequency does not come from ingesting psychedelics alone but rather requires daily dedication to your thoughts, words, and behavioral patterns in the same way making healthy dietary choices meal after meal helps you to naturally shed pounds.

As you have high-frequency experiences, be mindful about nourishing your energy and giving new frequencies the opportunity to settle into you. Be patient with your progress and notice how you respond to new developments within yourself. If you do feel overwhelmed by too many changes too fast, then ask your Divine Team for help with balance and integration.

do it!

Here is a simple meditation for prayer and protection that you can do separately or add to the beginning of another meditation practice.

- Imagine yourself surrounded by white light. See it all around you— in front of you, behind you, to each side, above and below.

- Say silently or out loud, "I connect to my Higher Self."

- Ask to be protected and surrounded by only the highest benevolent beings.

- Bring your hands together in front of your heart center. Use your attention to let the energy grow in your heart center.

- Place your problems or someone you wish you help through prayer in your heart. See or imagine them wrapped in uplifting, high vibrational light, coming into balance and wholeness.

CHAPTER 5

WHO ARE YOU BECOMING?

Who you are right now is a result of all of the choices you have made up to this point. The food you've eaten, your level of physical activity over the years, and all the thoughts you have ever entertained have made you who you are today. The repetitive thoughts that have continuously looped through your mind have colored your perception of the world as safe, dangerous, exciting, scary, boring, beautiful, or hideous at different times throughout your life. Judgment and limiting or empowering beliefs about yourself and others have either held you back, prevented you from exploring certain life choices about relationships, love, and career, or propelled you to new horizons. Words that you have spoken have built or burned bridges. Actions you have taken have uplifted others or hurt them. Every single one of us is where we are now because of who we have been and what we have done in the past.

While we are the sum of our past choices, each now moment is a choice point for integrating who we are with who we are becoming. Envisioning a higher version of ourselves and who we wish to become sets the stage for the actions we take in the present moment to bring that higher version to bear.

So, the question is, who are you becoming?

Are you setting yourself up for great health in the future by making choices to keep your physical temple strong and healthy through physical activity, drinking plenty of pure water, and eating vibrant food that nourishes your cells? Or are you stressing your physical body by not giving it the love and care it needs to support you in the best way possible?

What about your thought patterns? Are you making a habit of thinking higher vibrational thoughts to improve your mental well-being? Are you noticing thought patterns that are harmful or low vibration and diligently choosing to replace those with a new thought of a higher truth? If you are cutting gossip out of your verbal diet, your words will be more aligned with integrity and higher truth, and you will be spending much less time in lower-vibrational conversations that draw lower-vibrational thoughts and experiences to you.

What choices are you making to support your spiritual growth? Are you engaging in meditation, journaling, or other spiritual practices to align with higher aspects of yourself? Consuming high-vibrational content such as uplifting music, books, and podcasts, and the many other suggestions given throughout this book, create new neural pathways and networks that open you to new, higher perspectives about the reality in which you find yourself.

Who are you becoming?

LOOKING GLASS

Your experience of the external world is a reflection of you.

I have heard this saying tossed around over the years, but it wasn't until I had my own multidimensional experience of a quantum realm of mirrors that I understood this concept at a deep, visceral level of knowing. Immersed in a mystical state, I saw reflective geometric shapes that I understood were actually people from my physical reality in normal waking consciousness. The geometric shapes came together into a shape reminiscent of a person. Rather than seeing the other person coming into view, the geometric shapes comprising the human form were reflective. No matter the angle, all I could see was a kaleidoscope of tiny reflections of myself.

From this experience, I gained a powerful insight that every time I think I am interacting with another, I am actually witnessing a reflection of myself.

Another way of understanding this is that what we perceive in the external world is a direct reflection of us as the observer. What appears to be external, outside of us, is directly influenced by the observer, inside of us.

I am always very grateful for the wisdom that comes through in my multidimensional experiences, yet this particular insight carries a little sting. What if someone makes me angry or I am faced with a great challenge? Knowing this is reflective of me on some level creates a degree of personal accountability that's not easy to confront. I want to be able to point my finger at the other, signaling it's their fault and absolving myself of any responsibility. I mean, really, *how dare they*!

Admitting that reflection when things get hairy remains mastery-in-progress. It can be very evident that there is work yet to do on my inner self when things start to go sidewise *out there*. I still have interactions that make me think, *Man, what a jerk!* And obviously, the jerk is the other guy, not me, because I'm never a jerk. Right? RIGHT?

But at least I am aware of the challenge of finding that part of myself reflected in the observation or interaction. If someone triggers me, it is because I am focusing on what I see in them that is not yet resolved within myself. Things I find annoying in another reflect qualities about myself that I don't like. Even if I don't exhibit their behaviors outwardly, the shadow is still held deep within me. What I see that I don't like stirs a resonance with matching, unresolved energy within myself that I don't want to acknowledge consciously. Without the trigger, I wouldn't see this hidden part of me. Like it or not, the experience is illuminating an important area for growth when I am ready.

On the flip side, things I admire in others might be gifts I have not yet developed within myself. The greatness I can witness in someone else resonates with untapped greatness somewhere deep within me.

Love the One You're With, YOU!

In a truly multidimensional fashion, another lesson baked into my realm of mirrors experience is the importance of self-love. A hallmark of Western culture is a distorted sense of modesty and deference that encourages us to put ourselves last. We have an epidemic of low self-worth that permeates all levels of our culture. The average person is perpetually plagued by thoughts of shame, guilt, grief, regret, and other low-frequency thoughts stemming from a sense of separation and comparison of self to others, be that at an individual or collective level. There are myriad ways we have been programmed with the message of living up to prescribed standards of conduct, appearance, and servitude coming from family, religion, school, the workplace, and, in more recent years, through the ubiquitous presence of social media.

That's a lot of opportunity to find all the ways you don't measure up, resulting in an endless cycle of self-defeating thoughts. Low self-esteem, whether simply putting other needs before your own or a deep sense of shame and anything in between, directly contradicts the high-frequency thoughts of self-empowerment and unconditional love that are our true nature. More importantly, our ability to love others requires that we first love ourselves. How can we love our neighbor as ourselves when we are unable to love ourselves?

Unconditional love is a powerful energy that supplies us with the vital life force that flows into every area of our life—body, mind, and soul. When we love ourselves, we tune into the potent, high-frequency energy of love and allow it to flow unabated throughout our being. When we embody love, we then see that love in others. Because what we see in another are reflections of ourselves, the more we work on loving and accepting ourselves, the more we will be able to love and accept another. Letting love take up residence within us allows it to overflow to others.

Leo Tolstoy aptly captured the profundity of this way of understanding how we literally change the world from within. He said, "Everyone thinks of changing the world, but no one thinks of changing himself."[12] As we explored earlier, what we observe in the external world is influenced by us as observers. When we embody the frequency of love, that is the reflection we see in our perception of others and the world around us. It stands to reason that, in turn, when you are looking upon another with love, you are also lifting them to the love frequency at a quantum level, whether they are aware of it or not. Simply by observing something with love, it is automatically infused with that love. Working on yourself to bring in more loving energy allows you to change everything and everyone you see into a higher-frequency version.

Have you ever noticed how different it feels to be you in the presence of people who are emanating a strong force field of love? Just being around someone who is embodying the love frequency cultivates an amazing feeling of calm and upliftment. This is because they have worked on configuring their inner state in such a way that they change what they are observing. When you are in their presence, you are a part of their outer reflection. Your inner state rearranges in resonance with their high frequency, allowing you to feel more love flowing through yourself.

THE GAIN OF LOSS

We attract to us the level of frequency that we are emanating. Like attracts like. As we raise our frequency, we see new people, experiences, and things show up in our lives that are in harmony with our vibe.

Not only do new people come into our experience, but the more negative and less life-affirming people in our lives fall away. We are naturally no longer drawn to the same friends when our frequency rises, but their frequency remains unchanged. While there can certainly be heartache and a sense of loss when relationships dissolve or end angrily, this can be a natural and necessary part of becoming a higher version of ourselves.

We begin to see the world around us with fresh eyes that reveal how certain people with negative, low vibrational frequency perspectives and behaviors drag us down or influence us to see life through a similar dim lens. Until we have this expanded awareness, we may have never connected that their negativity had become our negativity.

As we begin to open ourselves up and focus on raising our vibration, we become more sensitive to the energy of others. There may be an energetic heaviness in our interactions with others who are operating at a lower frequency than our own, leaving us feeling weighted down, drained, or emotionally triggered. As we begin to understand how much the lower vibrational energy of negative thinking adversely impacts our spiritual growth and expanding consciousness, spending less time around people who drag us into a lower vibrational frequency is imperative, if not inevitable.

Believe me when I say that stepping away from friendships and relationships that are no longer aligned with our spiritual awakening is not always easy. At times, I wondered if the loss and drama of letting go were worth releasing myself from the throes of the friendship. For me, it was, but there is certainly a cautionary tale of the dedication it can take to stay the course of our awakening journey.

As we detach from friends and family who are no longer aligned with our journey, the emotional whiplash of holding firm to a path of spiritual growth can be daunting. For me, there was nostalgia for past good times and the FOMO moments when I thought about the fun and connection I was missing out on by letting the friendship dissolve. Then there was just plain old sadness and grief over the loss of a once dear friend, even though I knew *it was for the best*. Weaved into all of that was some outrage, bursts of anger, and painful regret as I took stock of all that brought me to the point of dissolution in the first place. These experiences have been humbling and courageous adventures that attest to the adage that what doesn't break you makes you stronger.

This aspect of personal relationships changing as our frequency changes is a rite of passage for many. Ultimately, the relationships that shift or dissipate are opportunities to come into gratitude, appreciation, forgiveness, and compassion, releasing us to move into more aligned relationships. Remember, like attracts like. As you continue to raise your vibrational frequency, people who will be in more harmonious resonance with you will undoubtedly show up.

RE-SLAYING THE DRAGON

Maturing along the spiritual path takes diligence and work, continually refining yourself. While there may initially be a sense of urgency and enthusiasm to heal every wound and gain every insight all at once to make up for lost time, it is far more important to take a measured approach. Each rock looked under, or layer of the onion peeled back, exposes truths about yourself, some more startling than others. Knowing and accepting yourself at each stage of revelation is vital. It's not a race to surface all of your flaws in thought, word, and action and risk drowning with regret and self-loathing over a past you cannot change.

Rather, the spiritual path is one of a curious traveler who takes time to stop and appreciate the journey for its own sake. It's about courageously and impartially noticing how you interact with the world now, in each moment, recognizing the vulnerabilities that bring you into lower frequencies, and actively cleaning them up. It's a continuous process of creating yourself.

What's truly wonderous is how the unfolding is never more than we can handle. As we open to new depths of healing, insight, and wisdom, the next level of refinement is illuminated in an ongoing process of spiritual growth and expanding consciousness. You may think you've resolved an issue, only to see it resurface. It's like an air bubble under a pool cover: push it down in one spot, and it pops up in another. Push it down again, and it appears elsewhere. However, with diligence and patience, you can eventually work the air bubble to the edge where it can be released forever.

Self-mastery takes practice, and it is only through repeated opportunities to slay our dragons that we eventually do so for good. Sometimes, a dragon we thought was mortally wounded shows up again, setting an unresolved issue on fire. We may be in the middle of fighting that same darn dragon all over again before we realize its familiarity. The courageous spiritual warrior keeps going. We observe our patterns and recognize when the same issue arises disguised as new circumstances. We are diligent and patient as we work toward acceptance and neutrality.

Everyone who has ever been on a path of self-mastery has had to re-slay the same dragons over and over again. For instance, we may have come out of a relationship that triggers anger when we remember being manipulated. This is an opportunity to meditate on compassion for everyone involved as an immediate antidote to feelings of anger or defensiveness. But additional work might be needed to clear the core wounds and shadow energy related to the trigger. It may be frustrating to find that we *still* feel triggered even with all that work. It's okay. That just means this is a gift that will keep on giving until we have alchemized all the fire of our inner dragon into deep transformation and inner strength.

Speaking from personal experience, the transformative work of confronting emotional triggers head-on is not for the faint of heart. In my experiences, working through emotional triggers has been a journey of turbulent emotions and powerful revelations about myself that had nothing to do with those who had ignited my trigger except the gifts they gave me to learn to love myself.

SHIFTING INTO THE NEXT VERSION OF YOURSELF

Who you are is not fixed. You may have held your beliefs very tightly and exhibited certain behaviors for as long as you can remember. But at any moment, you can discover higher truths and embody different behaviors and responses to what shows up in your life. Don't be afraid to change. To grow is to change. To evolve is to change.

Lower frequency thought patterns that keep us from realizing higher versions of ourselves and connecting with our higher selves have been inherited through ancestral lines, reinforced through the media, drilled in through religious dogma, and more. But we are not at the mercy of those forces. Through awareness, courage, and dedication, we make new choices, creating higher patterns of thought and behavior. What you are doing now shapes who you will be in the future. Be diligent about making higher choices so the new neural connections they create will get stronger and more dominant.

If you are making the same choices now that you were six months ago, then expect very little growth in the coming six months. Being stuck in the same thought patterns about your limitations, the hardships you have endured, the people who have done you wrong, jealousies, heartbreak, injuries, loss— the list goes on—reinforce old patterns and habits that keep you from making greater strides in your development.

Firmly holding onto patterns of your past doesn't leave any space for change. Instead, loosening your grip and consciously using negative thoughts and experiences as mirrors that reflect where you are stuck and need to clear out old energies and thought patterns invites positive change toward a new, higher version of yourself.

Support yourself in becoming the highest version of yourself through your choices.

Flipping the Script

We live in a world of duality. Everything in our human experience has its opposite—male-female, up-down, left-right, hot-cold, cloudy-sunny, and, of course, right and wrong. While opposites are a fundamental part of our physical experience, they do not apply to our spiritual world. Duality is an illusory tool for our human experience.

We experience life through the filter of good and bad, positive and negative experiences. We want what we believe to be positive and repel the negative. However, considering the whole scope of our lived experiences, the strongest lessons and biggest growth often come from the experiences we call negative. These most challenging moments of our lives also offer the most powerful gifts of compassion, honesty, generosity, love, and forgiveness from being one who has grieved deeply, been cheated, betrayed, or trespassed, lived in lack, and suffered from love withheld. So, while we have all had experiences that have been traumatic and painful, the fullness of who we are is the sum of everything we have been through and what we have overcome.

You cannot control what life throws at you. But you are in control of how you respond and what you think about those challenges. Instead of seeing your life as something happening to you, consider all your experiences as opportunities and know that all experiences, even the negative ones, hold important gifts for propelling you into the next, higher version of yourself.

So, again, who are you becoming? Are you still the same person who gets impatient when people are late, or can you flip your perception to embrace the unexpected pocket of time to recenter yourself and breathe? Do you relish the opportunity to point out your neighbor's flaws, or can you catch yourself in that outdated behavior and find a different thread to pull in the conversation?

Do you get angry and frustrated when someone is bound in religious dogma, or do you stretch yourself to sympathize with the programming they have not yet worked their way out of? Are you quickly insulted, or can you shift into giving the benefit of the doubt? Do the accomplishments of a peer make you dizzy with jealousy, or can you find the higher expression of genuine happiness for their success? Are you holding yourself back out of fear, or are you living in the safety of the ever-present moment?

The Pause

Giving pause between an emotional trigger and the emotional reaction is critical for creating new response patterns that, in turn, create new neural pathways for becoming your best self. Rather than falling into a reactive state, take time to notice what has happened. Notice the emotional reaction welling up inside you, then pause to acknowledge the feeling while taking a few deep belly breaths to calm and shift your focus inward; allow each breath to bring a deeper sense of grounding and centeredness.

Remain in this inner space until the momentary intensity of your emotional response has passed. From that space of inner quiet, notice your authentic self, not the knee-jerk reaction, and move into a state of acceptance that allows you to respond to the situation from a higher, more refined perspective. Pay attention to even the smallest emotional reaction as an opportunity to practice refining your response. Keep noticing your responses and reactions and refine them when you are getting pulled into the lower-frequency thoughts and emotions.

This pause was one of the early benefits I received from meditation. My more impulsive reactions to triggers were gradually replaced by more mindful and deliberate responses. Does this mean I never get triggered anymore? It does not; I'm still human, and my emotions can still flare up sometimes. I live with teenagers, for goodness' sake! Talk about some unrelenting mirrors. But I am much less susceptible to outbursts of anger than I was before I adopted a meditation practice.

You may find you have ample opportunities to work on your reactions to being triggered! Life is funny that way. Extend compassion to yourself as you develop the habit of recrafting your typical reactions into more measured and heart-based responses. Over time, the patience, compassion, and grace you once had to conjure up actively will become your default.

Authentically compassionate and harmonious responses reflect a higher frequency state of being. As your frequency increases, you attract fewer situations that trigger you. *Why?*

Is that because you aren't so easily triggered? In other words, what used to throw you into emotional turmoil no longer has that same power over you and now barely registers as a blip on your radar when it floats in.

Is that because lower-frequency experiences simply can't appear in your higher-frequency field? Without a matching lower-frequency energy field, there is no place for low-frequency energy to land. Nothing is magnetizing it to you; it's unwelcome and doesn't even reach your door. Operating at a higher frequency attracts higher experiences.

So, the answer is, it's both!

Creating New Patterns

You have the power to create the next version of yourself. You are not at the mercy of life. You always have choices, even if you have always believed there is one way to live, react, make a living, or be in relationships.

We construct our lives by telling ourselves remarkably convincing stories about reality. We perpetuate perceived limitations throughout our day—I'm not good with numbers; I hate running; I'm not creative; I'm unlovable; they don't want me to come; they're hanging out without me; I'm not good enough; I'm not smart; I'm always distracted;

I could never eat healthily; I'm not strong enough; I can't live without them; I always have to be busy; I could never resist alcohol, meat, sugar. I could go on, and so could you. The point is we subconsciously reinforce these limitations by perceiving each new situation through the same lens that supports a limited view of self. Take a moment to absorb the profundity of this simple truth.

We subconsciously reinforce our limitations each time we view a new opportunity through the same old lens.

Scientific research calls this phenomenon confirmation bias. Studies conclude that humans favor and trust information that confirms what we already believe or value. We literally filter out information that doesn't match what we already think or understand. Things that don't fit into our box will be essentially invisible to us, misunderstood, or not trusted.

Opportunities continuously arise to create new ways of being, and each time we meet a new experience with our limited confirmation bias, we reinforce our old patterns. For instance, if we have a lifelong view that we aren't good at math, we instinctually pull the mental file of limitation that says math is confusing whenever we encounter anything related to math. We feel overwhelmed with a flurry of mental activity before we even try to work through the problem. Perhaps we give up altogether and hand off the problem to someone else: *Twenty percent off? You do the math; I'm worthless with numbers!* Shrug.

Alternatively, we can employ the power of choice and choose not to accept the limiting belief, throw off the worn-out lens, and see ourselves anew. It might take a big belly breath to calm your nerves and center yourself, along with a dose of patience while you take the time to make the calculation, but it's an opportunity to strike gold on your journey to becoming your best self. Taking deep breaths gets the nervous system under control and settles down the chaotic brain activity that spikes in response to the challenge, providing more clarity and focus. From that place, the solution comes much more easily. As you experience this new version of yourself conquering your math limitation, you create a new pattern and neural network that begins to redefine who you think you are.

Twenty percent off? I've got this!

Miracle in Healing Waters

My friend and mentor, Michael, has a remarkable example of the power of releasing limiting beliefs, which he described in episode 118 of my *Soul Elevation* podcast.

Michael's story of overcoming limiting beliefs began when he visited a spot called Healing Waters with his friend named Socrates; for me, as the mamma of a precious cat named Aristotle, any story involving someone called Socrates immediately grabs my interest! As they were chatting in the beautiful surroundings, Michael mentioned that he had been dealing with chronic inflammation in his hand due to a splinter that had been embedded in his pinky finger for about a year and a half. Every month or so, the finger would swell up painfully, and Michael would try to remove the splinter to no avail.

With a little chuckle at the coincidence, Socrates confided that he had a similar experience with a piece of glass that had stubbornly embedded in his thumb. It took years, but eventually, his body expelled the tenacious glass out of the tip of his thumb.

While sitting by their campsite fire the next day, Michael noticed a dark spot on the affected pinky finger and, on closer examination, realized it was the wood splinter surfacing from its hidden lair. It was sticking out just enough to grab it with his fingernails and pull it out completely. Relief!

Almost as an act of permission, Socrates had given Michael a new perspective that allowed him to think differently about his problem. Until then, Michael believed that if a splinter did not naturally expel in a couple of weeks, it never would. Without a new belief to shatter the old one, he was as stuck as the splinter in his finger. But his reality shifted within hours of releasing his grip on a mistaken belief. The splinter had served its purpose of showing him the power of beliefs and our associated version of reality.

We are naturally dynamic and ever-changing, ever-expanding beings. If you feel stuck or constrained from growing and expanding, take an honest look at the barriers and obstructions of your own mental constructs and belief system that may be at the root of your impasse. These limitations we place on ourselves can be very sneaky and so well-entrenched that we don't see them right away. Unearthing our limiting beliefs to allow the truth of who we are to shine through is an ongoing process. Thankfully, opportunities will continue to present to work through our perceived limitations until we have aligned our thinking with the next higher version of ourselves, where we will find new opportunities for learning, expansion, and growth.

STAYING SMALL FOR OTHERS

One of the major barriers to expressing a higher version of ourselves is succumbing, consciously and subconsciously, to the familiar expectations of others at the cost of our true self. We don't want our partners, parents, friends, or colleagues to see us change and judge us for it. We feel they expect us to be consistent with who we have always been. In turn, we also find safety and comfort in the familiarity we have with others and theirs with us.

Those first steps into exploring our spiritual nature require us to step away from what is familiar and likely outside the conventional thinking of those we interact with regularly. At the beginning of expanding into new ways of thinking and living, we are in unfamiliar territory. The new beliefs and behaviors we are exploring are not time-tested in our lives or in the lives of those we know; we are in uncharted terrain that can make us feel insecure. This leaves us with no choice but to move into our expansion without a written script and instead turn to our inner knowing and faith in what can be when we shift into a higher frequency.

Still, even though we may have a deep knowing about our path and the changes needed to become a higher version of ourselves, initially, there is much preparation to set the stage for this new version of ourselves to make its entrance. Anchoring the truth of your authentic expression as a gravitational force to prevail over the expectations of others is crucial. Upholding the old you to make others comfortable will make it extremely difficult—nay, impossible— to begin making the changes necessary for the new you to arrive and take center stage.

Always remember whose life you are living. You are not living your life for anyone else, plain and simple. Worrying that you won't be accepted if you change is no excuse. Regardless of who might be threatened by your changes, you are not living their life, and they are not responsible for your life. Your purpose is not to please anybody else by the way you decide to live your precious life.

Some people may not support your positive changes simply because they don't understand them. When you are not the same you, you have disrupted the status quo of your relationships with others in ways that may threaten their beliefs and ways of operating.

If you used to bond with your friends by excessive drinking on the weekend and then you have no interest in alcohol, your friends may subconsciously feel rejected and project that onto you as accusations of being superior or some other character flaw. So be mindful of the possibility that those who are not ready to change might throw stones at you in defense of their choices.

Just as others are a mirror of your inner world, you are also a mirror reflecting back to others their inner worlds. Your growth may be an unwelcome trigger for others because it surfaces something uncomfortable for them to look at. Understanding this, you can extend compassion for any misguided accusations while honoring your awakening and the changes in your life.

Knowing the intricacies and depth of emotion that change of any kind can provoke, it's important to be especially mindful of how you talk about your own growth and change. However well-intentioned, even the smallest implication that you have chosen a higher path can easily spark a defensive response when someone is not open and ready to celebrate the opportunity for growth. Take time to consider how you can explain your choice to operate at a higher vibration without implying that others are at a lower vibration that no longer aligns with yours.

Highlighting someone else's opportunities for growth when they are not looking for your honest opinion on the matter is patently unwise. For one, we never know what is truly best for others and how their soul journey is playing out in their best and highest good. We are not in any position to be in judgment about what's a growth opportunity for someone else. Second, what may seem like priceless advice for another's spiritual or personal growth will probably be received as a personal attack, especially if it is clear they have chosen a lower-frequency landscape for their life lessons.

Stay focused on your own work, make the best choices for your life, and respect others and their choices. Don't engage with negative thinking or reactions that arise for others in response to the changes in you. Resist pointing out any limiting beliefs you notice in their reaction. Keep it clean by focusing on you.

Our level of sacrifice for our expansion is an individual choice that is not black-and-white.

Are you willing to undergo the discomfort of disappointing someone else to pursue your spiritual development, or are the expectations of others your priority? There is no absolute answer. It is a matter of the priority we give to our expansion and growth in each circumstance. We are never required to conform to anyone's expectations. But even if we have chosen to conform year after year after year, we can make a different choice today, now, or at any point in the future. Every moment of every day is a choice point. Ultimately, no one else—not even our spouses or those closest to us— is responsible for our embodiment of a higher frequency. Alignment with our life's purpose is an inside job only we can take on. If you want spiritual growth, you must make the choices that allow that growth to take root and thrive. Brick by brick, day by day, choice by choice: this is how you become aligned with your Higher Self.

KIDDING OURSELVES

Spiritual bypassing is the propensity to outwardly project a higher emotional state than we actually feel because we don't want to be perceived as engaging with low vibrational energy. We plaster on the tight-lipped, wide-eyed smile that everything is A-OK! when on the inside, we are boiling with anger, sadness, or hurt. Spiritual bypassing is dangerous territory that can quickly devolve into a deluded state of spiritual superiority and, worse, to total separation from your authenticity, which is your primary gateway for connecting with your Higher Self.

Key to aligning with your Higher Self is not kidding yourself about who you have become.

As we navigate the myriad changes in ourselves and our lives through living a higher-frequency life, we must hold sacred our authentic experience of it and not put on a mask of serene calm when we are exploding with emotions. Of course, I'm not suggesting being inconsiderate of others by unleashing the beast, so to speak. But it is critical to feel our true feelings without denying them so they can pass through us. If we have an unpleasant emotion and try to pretend it away, the energy of the emotion becomes trapped within our energy fields.

Emotions are energy; ideally, our energy moves freely and harmoniously through our mind-body-spirit complex. But when we refuse to acknowledge our emotions, they are not processed through this system and stay stuck, buried, and hidden at the subconscious level. When our conscious mind rejects authentic emotions, it creates a mismatch, sometimes called disassociation, within our system. The mismatch between our conscious and subconscious mind and the pent-up emotional energy become energy densities that cause blockages and stagnation. Densities in our energy fields ultimately become vulnerabilities that make us more prone to disease, mental instability, and injuries.

We may fear that we will *become* that emotion if we give in to it. Especially in the heat of the moment when we have been triggered, it can feel as though we *are* anger as opposed to *feeling* anger. But we must remember that emotions are temporary; they are not who we are. Just a few moments of deep breathing to calm the mind can quickly reveal the passing nature of even an extreme emotional response.

In her book *My Stroke of Insight*, Dr. Jill Bolte-Taylor talks about how it only takes 90 seconds for the chemical process caused by an emotion to complete its cycle through the body.[13] After a minute and a half, the chemical reaction of the emotion is completely flushed out of the bloodstream, and the automatic response is over. But we know from experience that an emotion can feel as though it lasts much, much longer—even extending into years or decades when left unchecked.

When we continue to feel the fear, anger, or sadness of an event after that initial chemical processing, we are actually re-stimulating our circuitry and creating the physiological response over and over again. At this point, our thoughts, not the experience itself, are creating the emotional response. The body, nervous system, and mind behave just as though the experience is happening again in this moment. We are bringing the past pain into the present moment each time we ruminate over difficult experiences we've had. We sacrifice the safety and potential of the moment in order to relive painful experiences and put our bodies through the same taxing process time and again.

With spiritual maturity, we become less overtaken by our emotional responses. We feel and accept our feelings and take responsibility for them to the best of our ability. We accept that we cannot control another's actions toward us, but we are responsible for our response. We acknowledge when we are feeling unpleasant emotions like fear, anger, or jealousy and give ourselves the pause and space to be able to *respond* from a place within that is aligned with a higher frequency rather than to *react* in a primal way.

Remember the 90-second chemical process you undergo when hit with an emotionally charged event. Feel that process, notice it, be aware of the change within you, and breathe. Bring awareness and acceptance to how you feel. Invoke your ability to just be without reacting or lashing out. Through that pause, you can begin to process your emotions authentically without denying them, and you create a platform from which you can respond in a more productive way.

- Take some time to think about what version of yourself you would most like to step into. Break out your journal and write down a description of this higher version of yourself.

  What have they overcome?

  What have they forgiven?

  How are they spending their time?

- Next, brainstorm some actions that form the bridge from who you are now to that version of yourself.

  Is that higher version of you more patient, less stressed, calmer?

  Is the higher version of yourself a healer?

  Is the next version of you surrounded by like-hearted people who encourage your spiritual development and reflect back to you the reality you want to be living?

Push yourself to focus on what you can do to carry you into who you want to become.

You could add a regular meditation practice to reduce stress and improve your patience, calm, and focus. Perhaps you could enroll in a course to develop your healing gifts or join an online or in-person community focused on an area of interest that excites you.

Once you have created some actionable ideas, the next suggestion might be really *out there,* but stay with me:

Take those actionable ideas and actually do them!

Create a meditation practice. At the end of the book, you will see an Invitation to Connect page, where you will find a link to my online courses that include meditation practices. Learn more about healing if that's your thing. Take an art or dance class to express yourself more creatively. Join and participate in a local or online community.

If you just keep these ideas as thought forms and don't actually do anything with them, put down this book, look in the mirror, and say hello to the version of you who will be staring back at you in six months. Be the creator of your life. Shake off all the hardened, crusty thoughts, habits, and beliefs from the past and start creating tomorrow's version of yourself right now.

CHAPTER 6

BANISHING FEAR

Release. Your. Fear.

Fear is a low-frequency vibration. It inhibits expansion and perpetuates more fear in our lives. Fear energy contracts and constricts our energy field, leaving us vulnerable to negative experiences and emotions.

Fear triggers our nervous system's fight-or-flight response, creating a sense of alarm and urgency that takes our mental state out of peace and neutrality. Physiologically, the fight-or-flight response prevents major organs such as our hearts, lungs, and digestive system from receiving nourishment and energy as the body directs its resources to the senses and extremities to prepare for quick action.

Despite all the ways that fear energy negatively affects our minds, bodies, spiritual expansion, and life experiences, releasing it is no easy task. It is one of the biggest hurdles we must overcome to increase our vibrational frequency and connect with higher consciousness, including the Higher Self. Many reasons at both the personal and collective level contribute to the depth of our addiction to fear, the most compelling of which is the extent to which we have completely normalized it in our society. We are fed fear ad nauseam all day long. Just spend a few minutes listening to the news cycle, and you'll probably feel your body react to the onslaught of countless stories of the latest thing to worry about.

Each time we engage with the harmful scenarios the news feeds us, our nervous systems take a hit. We don't just watch the TV with our eyes. Our whole bodies come along for the ride as the sympathetic nervous system's fight-or-flight response is activated. Even without being truly in danger, the powerful imagination invokes responses in the body as though we are. Many studies show that your body response is similar whether you are personally experiencing something or just watching someone experience it.

So why put yourself through undo stress by watching the news and continuously opening the door to the daily traumas happening across the planet? Is it worth your well-being to be informed to the nth degree? What hits are your mental and even physical health taking in exchange for the perceived value of staying voraciously up to date on current events?

FREE THINKING

When we turn to a news outlet that feels reliable or neutral, it's likely reporting a narrative that aligns with our own values and perspectives, making it resonate within us as accurate. We become blind to the editorial slant in reporting because it feels true according to our worldview, reinforcing what we already believe. But whether we see it or not, there is always spin in the news we consume.

It is well known that the major news outlets have their own agendas about what is newsworthy, why, and what facts to cover. These agendas color every news story we see or hear. At each stage of the reporting process, from the investigation to the script and production, news staff have a line to tow and a slant to adhere to in the stories they report. Everyone answers to and is restricted by their superiors and the news corporation. Writers and editors create content based on directives handed down by their management team. Lower-level management reports to higher-level management and on up the chain until the news we consume has become a precisely distilled *story* about current events.

The livelihood of news media professionals is dependent upon them delivering broadcasts that fit in with the narrative or version of reality that that particular news outlet is trying to create, not to mention the psychological pressure humans feel to be accepted and respected by their colleagues in their work environment. News stories are not neutral facts; they are an interpretation of what has happened, and there are agendas to get you to buy into their particular interpretation.

Add to that the phenomenon that news has become increasingly entertainment-based for profit. Reporters, writers, editors, and producers know very well that fear drives viewership, and they infuse the news cycle with fear and sensationalism to keep people watching. News outlets thrive on selling a fear-based perspective, and the more you tune in, the more that perspective colors the lens through which you see reality. Fear keeps you clicking links and tuning into the latest updates that track with the perspective you have bought into. The more we click and follow the news, the more we get addicted to the need for more news to tell us what we need to know to feel safe.

It's easy to get sucked in by the lure that knowing more by staying on top of the news will provide the sense of security you are seeking. But it doesn't. Relying on more news to solve the problem of the fear and insecurity that it perpetuates is like eating sugar to lose weight. Breaking up with the news doesn't make you any less safe or secure, but it stops feeding your fear that you're not. With a little time and patience, removing the debilitating energy of the news feed frees you to find true peace and security through the improved sense of well-being that sprouts almost immediately when you simply tune out.

When I stopped regularly engaging with the news cycle, I found that removing the constant feed of fear programming from my life was extremely liberating on many levels. From the time it gave me back to focus on higher-frequency activities to a profound shift in my freedom of thought, it was nothing short of a revolutionary life change. Removing the talons of the news media from my energy fields has freed me to express and explore my own thoughts and opinions rather than regurgitate what the talking heads are spouting.

If It Happened to Them...

More than anything on the TV screen, the perpetual fear energy locks us into a lower frequency, stressing our bodies and hijacking our nervous system, creating untold damage. Consider a news segment showing images of a home that's been ransacked. Watching as the camera pans the scene, it's an automatic response to start running scenarios of how this might happen to you and your home. The list of possible vulnerabilities and how to protect yourself and your family grows from how a thief might gain entry to any manner of terrible things that might occur under your roof.

But there are no quick fixes, and a gnawing fear grows that you are more unprepared and vulnerable than you thought. Worse, before you've come to terms with that nightmare scenario, a new one comes along in the next story, showing a couple in financial ruin from identity theft. Rinse and repeat: the cycle of fear continues.

Commercials are no break from the fear cycle, as they are carefully tailored to manipulate you psychologically into feeling that danger lurks around every corner. Big pharma spends billions on ads to keep you in fear of contracting a debilitating condition or rare disease, most of which you have never even heard of before you saw the commercial. Worse, the side effects often sound worse than the medical condition: irritable bowel or death by the prescription drug—not a happy choice!

Insurance companies spend billions on ads exploiting accidents and disasters to send you reeling in fear to buy their product, even though you know any relief you may get through an insurance claim is likely its own unmitigated corporate assault, pouring proverbial salt in the wound. It's an endless barrage. On TV, it's all about what's happening to others. But if it happened to them, maybe you're next.

That's Entertainment?

What we consume as entertainment through streaming or broadcast television is an even greater source for feeding our fear addiction. I used to be drawn to true and fictional crime shows that recreate and dissect unspeakable and unlikely crimes, often perpetrated on the good-natured mom next door. This unsuspecting woman lives in the suburbs with her husband, two kids, a couple of cats, and a dog. She's got brown hair, loves lattes, and hails from a similar alma mater. Her name is probably Kara.

"Huh, look at that; she's just like me," says the voice in your head, then mutters on. "Never would have thought such a terrifying fate awaited her. She never saw it coming! There's probably a killer in my house, too. He could be behind me right now!"

Perhaps you are watching the news or fear-based entertainment at night when your body is naturally preparing for sleep. The hormones and chemicals running through your body at that time make you particularly susceptible to suggestion, amplifying the proposition that you are unsafe.

I often had difficulty sleeping when I regularly watched fear-based entertainment on TV, especially if my husband was traveling. I was afraid some terrible crime would happen while I was frolicking around in my dreams. Wherever would I have gotten that idea? By choosing to watch crime shows, I filled my head with all sorts of violent potentialities that seeped into my imagination and worried me when I was alone. I sleep so much better since I realized I was inviting fear with those choices and decided to favor more lighthearted entertainment.

Being careful about your media intake is low-hanging fruit for releasing fear. We are what we consume. Stop consuming fear and see what happens.

Fear by Any Other Name

Fear goes by many names.

Hello, stress! Unpack your stress a bit, and you will tend to find the core of it is fear.

Hi, anxiety! Notice your anxiety; follow its thread. Many times, anxiety is related to fear about the future.

Howdy, worry! Worry is the rumination of our fears and the endless ways they could become reality.

Notice when you feel out of balance in some way. Bravely be curious about it and discover what is driving that feeling. If you find fear, acknowledge it rather than deny it, take some breaths, and determine if it is serving you. Is it really something you need to be afraid of, or is it something that has come and gone that you survived and probably gained some key lessons from? Or is it some future potentiality that you are worried about and likely will never actually come to fruition?

Consider the astounding number of future potential scenarios you have been afraid of that never came to pass. Your future is full of untold possible outcomes, and most of those outcomes won't become manifest reality. Even if the worst possible scenario you can dream up does come, are you helping yourself at all by mulling it over now, or are you sacrificing what could be a neutral or even pleasant moment in exchange for projecting yourself into that unset future?

For the most part, we are comfortably safe and secure in the present moment. What makes us feel unsafe are projections about future calamity or reliving past trauma. A key, fundamental element to overcoming fear is present-moment awareness. As you read these words, you are not in any immediate danger. If you were in immediate danger, you would not have prioritized reading this. Instead, you would be in the throes of a dangerous situation. However, if you bring to mind something stressful happening in your life – a looming deadline, a recent argument, or an upcoming medical procedure – you bring that fear into this moment even though that stressful thing is not actually happening right now.

Be not afraid. We can reclaim our power and energy when we truly come into the present moment.

BAKED-IN FEAR

We live in an environment that deliberately uses fear as a form of control. It takes dedicated, concentrated effort to overcome this powerful and pervasive manipulation. Fear is so baked-in and entrenched in our society that it has become normalized, almost completely blinding us to its presence.

Here's a simple everyday example of what I mean by baked-in fear. As I was grabbing a shopping cart at my local supermarket, I noticed a sign above the cart corral area that said, "A safe child is a happy child." The sign provided information for ensuring safe practices regarding seating your child in the cart. On the surface, it is just a simple sign about the importance of keeping your kid out of danger, right? Let's go deeper and see what's really happening here.

To begin, the deeper message of this sign is this: the key to your child's happiness is keeping them safe. Failing to do that, you are a bad parent, and your children will be unhappy.

Many parents have a deep, innate desire for their children to be happy. So, a notice linking safety and happiness can highlight and agitate this for parents already trying to do their best. While I am not disputing the importance of our role as parents to act reasonably to protect our children from harm, I am questioning when that need to protect and make safe is so baked into every decision that it becomes the very definition of happiness, as the sign suggests.

It doesn't take much to imagine the many ways your child could become unsafe, underscoring the many ways you could fail to make your child happy. The inner dialogue ensues.

> *Sure, I'm doing what I can to protect my child from certain risks, but what about all the possible risks I haven't even considered? Am I doing everything I can to keep my child safe?*

After pausing to take a moment to tighten the cart strap, the inner dialogue continues.

> *What if I can't keep my precious child from getting hurt at some point? Not only will they be in pain, but they'll*

also be unhappy. Do I even really care about my child's happiness? What if I had not read the sign and forgot to strap them into the cart seat? Am I a bad parent?

That's a ton of responsibility on top of the enormous general responsibility of being a parent. It's scary being reminded that perhaps you haven't thought of every possible way to keep your child safe. Surely, you can do a better job of keeping your child safe and, therefore, happy. FEAR!

Perhaps you should spend more time and money trying to figure out how to be a better parent at the expense of expanding yourself and coming more fully into your purpose and gifts. FEAR!

Don't forget to be sure to continuously pass along the idea that safety is of paramount importance to your child's happiness so that your children can also grow up unconsciously limiting themselves in the misguided pursuit of their happiness by way of safety. BAKED-IN FEAR!

Also inherent to the statement that *a safe child is a happy child* is an agreement that *safety* is our number one priority and a precursor to happiness.

Safe = happy

Stay safe, stay happy. Strap your child securely in the cart and strap yourself securely into society. Play by the rules set out before you; keep your head down. Safe, secure, happy.

For safety to be our driving force, we must be aware of *all the risks* that threaten our safety. Those risks are scary. In most of life's decisions, the safest thing you can usually do is . . . nothing. You're safest hiding away and holding yourself back because getting out in the world and doing something, especially something new and unknown, has loads of risks and potential dangers.

But how happy are we *really* if we aren't stretching ourselves, learning, growing, and discovering?

What does that say about a view of happiness that doesn't include the kind of joy that awaits in blasting through limitations, figuring out something new, or experiencing the unknown? When we see happiness as nothing more than the avoidance of the risk of things we fear, we miss the opportunity to experience fulfillment and pleasure derived from our expansion and growth. It's worth questioning if we are mistaking a pristine life free of dents, bumps, bruises, or tears as truly fulfilling. Do we buy a set of beautiful dishes just to look at occasionally and never use, or do we enjoy the precious plates joyfully at every meal, understanding that through their use, they might get chipped? It seems to me that when it comes to happiness, we are much better off getting out of our comfort zones and using the beautiful dishes rather than staying small and comfortable.

While well-intentioned, overemphasizing safety leads to opting out of living. Being frozen in place because every potential step forward has an inherent potential risk means we will also never reap those gifts found only through experience.

A moment in the movie *Finding Nemo* perfectly sums this up.[14] Dory's friend Marlin can't find his son and feels terrible guilt for not keeping him out of harm's way.

Marlin says to Dory, "I promised I'd never let anything happen to him."

Dory replies, "Hmm. That's a funny thing to promise."

Marlin thinks about that and then asks Dory what she means.

"Well," says Dory, "you can't never let anything happen to him. Then nothing would ever happen to him."

Dory's right. Do we let fear stop us from enjoying life as it's happening, or do we freely engage with the world to explore and expand, knowing that stuff happens? I side with Dory. With a truly happy heart, you will always learn and grow from whatever happens, freeing your birth child and your inner child to be happy, grow, learn, expand, and experience the richness of life.

The Sign God

Back to the sign lording over the shopping cart area, another disturbing message is the idea that someone else—let's call them the Sign God—is an all-knowing purveyor of safety and happiness who decides what's best. This faceless, nameless authority confidently proclaims, as fact, that the pursuit of happiness stems from following instructions about how to be safe from all the fears about what could, and probably will, happen to make you unsafe. If left unchecked, we unquestionably agree with the Sign God and maybe even appreciate the sign as a friendly reminder of his omniscience, knowing it to be true because, well—it's written on a big sign!

I use the innocuousness of a shopping cart sign to illustrate how far-reaching and pervasive fear-driven agendas are, even in the most mundane moments of our daily lives. These fear agendas surreptitiously and continuously bombard us to the point that we just accept them as life as usual. In other words, fear has become unquestionably normalized.

But being in a state of constant fear isn't normal. It holds us back. It is holding us back as individuals, moving into a new expression of expanding consciousness and reclaiming our power, freedom, and sovereignty. Addiction to fear holds us back as a collective humanity from achieving these same goals when we agree to its iron grip, reinforcing fear-based living with each other and staying locked in a lower frequency.

What we believe, we perpetuate for better or worse. We give our energy to and strengthen the fears we cling to. We spread fears we haven't yet resolved within ourselves. We inherited fears from our family lineage that we continue to pass down the line when we haven't noticed and reconciled them within.

Fear = More Fear.

Happiness is not found in fear.

WHO WANTS YOUR FEAR?

Fear *literally* holds us in a lower vibration. Fear is an incredibly powerful instrument for anyone who wishes to keep us controlled and small. But who would want to control us, and why? Who has the power to control, and how do *they* benefit from keeping us in fear as a means of control?

Let's consider some of the usual suspects: corporations, governments, and, of course, the media conglomerates.

Again, we go back to another version of the safety equals happiness equation. Feeling unsafe or one of its low-frequency twins, insecure and vulnerable, makes us very susceptible to the proverbial *big brother*, who steps in with a solution to our perceived problem or need. Corporations and governments both respond to and even create these perceived needs.

Corporations thrive on our insecurity of not enough through advertising that agitates the feeling of lack that compels us to buy and consume their solutions. They are happy to supply the *more* that constantly feeds our illusory *lack*.

Governance thrives on our sense of powerlessness in the face of existential threats to national and local security. To make people feel powerless, feed them fear. The ever-present threat of invaders—human, viral or otherwise, and more—is easy pickings for governments to stoke fear, making us happy to comply and fall in line to protect ourselves, communities, and nations. Those who govern can be quick to supply more *protection* to feed our illusory *fear*, justifying ever-increasing controls and spending budgets, all in the name of security and patriotism.

We already looked at how media conglomerates benefit from selling fear because the more you are in fear, the more time you spend engaging with their programming, ratcheting up viewer numbers that feed their bottom line. More viewers means more advertiser dollars from corporations selling us goods and products to quench our need for *more,* bringing us back full circle to a deliberate fear cycle that we unwittingly play into.

Reclaiming Sovereignty

The highest option I see for resolving the pervasiveness and power of fear is for each of us to recognize what is happening and work to reclaim our sovereignty at the individual level, which then radiates out to the greater collective of humanity. We do this by identifying the manipulation we have endured by our steady intake of fear and then stepping out of the fear cycle into a higher vibrational reality that fosters our growth and expansion.

No longer buying into fear takes active work and choice. At first, it takes constant vigilance to recognize the subliminal fear-stoking baked into most messaging to the masses. Once we begin to see the face of fear almost everywhere we look, it quickly becomes tiresome to see the same old message, and eventually, we just patently refuse it. In its place, we find messages of upliftment and expansion for choosing a new narrative that we are creators of our reality who are lovingly supported by a benevolent Universe. We can then turn away from these external so-called authorities and make choices that align with our highest good, which in turn radiates out as the highest good for all.

_do it!_

Pick an area of your life to explore where your hidden fears may be buried. Getting pride and denial out of the way is essential for this exercise to take you anywhere. Be honest with yourself.

A helpful approach to this exercise is first to take a moment to get centered with a simple breathing meditation to focus your thoughts.

- Close your eyes.

- Take 3 deep breaths in and out of your nose.

- Scan your body from your toes up to your head and release any tension you feel along the way.

- Once you are centered, begin exploring hidden fears using the following suggestions. Identify some aspect of your life that consistently makes you feel stressed, worried, or anxious. Here are some common areas where that might come up for you.

o Raising a child

o Career aspirations

o Losing or never finding a partner

o Health goals

o Aging

o Finances

- Next, identify specific causes of your stress or worry in this area of your life. For instance, if your work situation is the biggest stress for you, identify all of the factors, like the ones listed below, that may be contributing to your stress and worry.

o Losing your job

o Don't like your colleagues

o Not enough income

o Don't enjoy the type of work

- Going deeper, there may still be another layer of subconscious fears. Identify what deeper fears may lie beneath the issues that came up for you in the previous step. Here are some underlying fears that may be related to the examples listed in the previous step.

o Stress of losing your job could point to the fear of running out of money or fear of unworthiness.

o   Stress from not getting along with colleagues can be rooted in a fear of judgment, not being accepted, or abandonment by your tribe.

o   Stress from not having enough income can be rooted in a fear of running out of resources.

o   Stress of not enjoying your work could indicate a core fear of being out of your life's purpose or wasting your gifts.

• Once you have identified the underlying fears, explore if there is any truth to them.

Are your underlying fears even a valid concern? Most likely, the odds are very small that any of them will ever even come to pass.

If any of these fears *did* materialize, can you trust that the tools and resources you would need to cope with that scenario would become available to you?

Even if such fear were to play out in your future, would it actually help you in this present moment to allow worry about that fear to consume what precious time you have?

Release all the fears, stress, and worries you have identified through the previous inquiries by utilizing this simple mediation.[15]

Acknowledge the fear identified through the previous steps.

Can you feel a place within your body that is holding this fear, such as a squeeze in your tummy, a tightness in your throat, or a contraction around your heart? It's ok if you can't find a physical response.

Whether or not you feel anything physically, say to yourself that you love and accept the parts of you that feel this fear.

Feel yourself really filling with love and acceptance for this part of you that carries fear. Don't try to push it away, deny it, or bury it. See it, feel it, accept it. Love into it.

Let the energy of your love and acceptance dissolve the energy of the fear.

When you feel that you have acknowledged, loved, and accepted the fears you have found, take a cleansing inhale through the nose and exhale through the mouth. Slowly open your eyes.

Because fear is so pervasive and hidden throughout society, this is a worthwhile exercise to practice regularly as we reorient ourselves out of fearful living. Unearthing and releasing our fears is an essential way to clear out lower vibrational energies so we can radiate frequencies more aligned with our Higher Self.

CHAPTER 7

THE HEART GATEWAY

You're ascending a mountain path when your guide suddenly stops and turns your attention to the surrounding landscape. At first glance, you don't see anything unusual. The brush, rocks, and dirt are unremarkable, leaving you wondering why you have stopped. But following your guide's urgings to still your mind and look more closely, you relax and notice the surface shifting into a shimmering surrealism. The hard, fixed dirt and rocks subtly transform into a permeable gateway, revealing a pathway leading inside.

As you gaze in awe at the brilliantly illumined path, your guide explains that this is a special route to higher consciousness. This gateway is always present just below the surface of ordinary reality, available for exploration whenever you give it your attention.

"Where did this gateway come from?" you quizzically ask your guide.

Without exchanging words, your entire body fills with a warm glow, and you *know* the answer— your heart. It's an instantaneous realization that your heart is an inner passageway to higher consciousness.

HEART BOSS

We connect to other humans—as well as other species and the energy of Earth herself—through the heart. From a multidimensional perspective, the heart is an inner gateway or portal to infinite possibilities. In my opinion, the heart is magic. And yet there it sits so innocently, right in the middle of our being. This powerful grail is hiding right in plain sight.

"Me, magic?" your sleeping heart whispers in response to your wonder.

Yes! The keys to opening enormous potential for spiritual awakening are within the heart.

For a long time, the brain was believed to send a one-way signal to the body, including the heart. However, recent research has revealed that the communication between the brain and heart is a two-way exchange. In fact, the heart sends even more signals to the brain than the brain sends to the heart.

The electromagnetic field coming from the heart is measurable using instrumentation, namely the electrocardiogram (ECG). Rollin McCraty, Ph.D., is a professor and director of research at the HeartMath Institute. According to Rollin's research, the heart emits an electrical field that is about sixty times greater than what the brain emits and a magnetic field more than 100 times greater than the brain's field. [16]

Other research from the HeartMath Institute shows that the heart's electromagnetic field is detectible several feet from the body.[17] This enhanced energy field helps us connect to other people and with all sentient life, such as animals, plants, the planet herself, and beyond. For example, when two people are in close proximity, their heart fields can combine into a detectible, united electromagnetic heart field. The heart's energy can even influence others from a distance.[18]

The electromagnetic energy from the heart that radiates outside of the body and influences others offers insights into the mysterious power of prayer. There are untold accounts of prayer having miraculous results. Perhaps you have your own experience with receiving or transmitting positive change through the power of heartfelt prayers.

Heart energy can even impact inanimate objects. After learning Reiki, a friend of mine was able to stop her refrigerator from making a loud noise by utilizing this heart-based healing art!

A Coherent Vibe

The HeartMath Institute has pioneered fascinating research quantifying how we influence others through our hearts. Through rigorous science over the past 30 years, they have developed tools and technologies for mastering heart energies by applying the principles of heart coherence.

According to the HeartMath Institute, heart coherence is a state of cooperative alignment between the heart, mind, emotions, and physical systems.[194] Coherence can be thought of as synergy. When our hearts and brains are in coherence, they work in harmony as one system. The more we attune with this alignment, the more the heart radiates a stronger, more coherent electromagnetic energy field.

Coherence supports the brain in functioning in a loving and compassionate way, resulting in brain waves that are steady and balanced rather than sporadic and uneven. The entire brain functions in a much more fluid, unified way rather than operating as isolated parts. The rhythmic brainwaves calm stress-producing patterns and enhance mental clarity, improving our ability to perceive and comprehend multidimensional intelligence coming through the heart.

Heart Frequency

Heart energy is a major player in the overall vibrational frequency we experience and emit. As science shows, the heart emits its own electromagnetic pulse that ripples throughout our entire body system and extends well beyond our physical form. It also works in alignment with other body systems and adapts to our emotional and mental states. As our overall frequency rises and lowers, the heart's frequency changes to match our vibrational state.

I have sometimes experienced a squeezing sensation in my heart associated with a change in my overall frequency. I'll feel a tight squeeze in my chest for a few moments, and then it will subside. The strongest experience of this squeezing I have felt was while driving with my friend Michael. We had just checked out a place where we would host our first retreat together and were riding a high vibe of excitement and purpose from being on those sacred grounds and tuning into the high energy of the future retreat. As we were leaving, I felt a sudden squeezing sensation in my chest. It felt like small electrical zaps in a specific place around my heart. I had to pull over and take some deep breaths to calm the sensation in my heart. The feeling passed after several minutes, and everything returned to normal.

The squeezing sensation can be uncomfortable, bringing up possible health concerns. However, knowing that every part of me is energy—including the physical aspects—I can shift my focus from panic to calm, releasing the constricted heart energy. When I experience this sensation, I deliberately shift into a neutral observation mode to determine if urgent medical attention is needed or if it's an energetic response to a sudden shift in vibrational frequency. So far, I have consistently found the constriction was attributable to a frequency shift related to an expansion of consciousness. I also don't have any pre-conditions to suggest a heart condition, but it's reassuring to pause and make the internal assessment.

By shifting to a higher frequency, my heart oscillated between the previous and the new frequencies. As my heart was stepping into the new frequency, the physical heart components were changing, which I experienced as a combination of electrical pulses and squeezing. Rather than *Bam! I was in one frequency a moment ago, and now and forever, I am in a higher one*; the process I experience is more of a flickering back and forth between the previous frequency and the new one until the new frequency and the associated expanded consciousness have fully settled in. The visceral heart sensations I experience occur during the flickering process.

Since first experiencing this, I have learned it is a known phenomenon, verified by Michael and other spiritual teachers. Carrying a new, higher frequency affects the whole of our being. Not only are we becoming more developed spiritually, but subsequently, all of our energy is shifting and expanding - emotionally, mentally, and even physically.

My only purpose in sharing this experience is simply to illustrate the close connection between our heart energy and overall frequency. I am not making any suggestions about how you may address a similar experience. We are all responsible for our health and must make the most appropriate decisions for ourselves.

TRAINING THE HEART

Developing the intuitive knowing of the heart is a critical crossroads on our spiritual journey, where we make a conscious choice to follow an inner path for connecting with higher consciousness. Unlike analytical knowing, intuitive knowing is based on intangible cues within the heart and body. The reasoning behind intuitive insights is often beyond the grasp of the rational mind.

Modern Western living tends to encourage us to override intuitive guidance from our hearts with rational direction from our analytical brains. Especially in the early stages of our awakening journey, intuitive knowing often runs counter to what our rational brains consider logical and practical, leading us to favor calculated, explainable, and quantifiable choices over what *feels* right in our hearts.

To quench our thirst for analytical certainty, we are driven to quantify everything possible into data points for calculated decision-making. This reminds me of a friend who was going through a difficult breakup with a very analytical partner. In an attempt to salvage their relationship, he created a detailed spreadsheet with a complicated scoring system to rate their relationship daily. Before my awakening on my spiritual path, I took a similar tactic, creating a data-driven analysis about moving from England to the US. No surprise: data points did not provide the answers in either case.

Using these kinds of analytical skills to understand and rationalize intuitive feelings is counterproductive. While pinning a data point to feelings and intuition may seem logical, the outcome of any such calculation misses the mark of the free-flowing surrender to the truth that lies within the unquantifiable. Trying to analyze and quantify feelings and intuition inherently takes us out of the heart and into the mind. To truly tune into the heart, we need to set the mind aside. The mind cannot do the heart's job properly, and we won't get answers the heart *knows* if we leave it out in the cold.

Quality Control

So, how do we find this gateway to higher consciousness via the heart's energy field and allow it to be stronger and more stable? Your heart reflects your emotional state and nervous system. Feeling stressed, angry, upset, scared, or nervous causes the heart to reflect with erratic, spiky, and incoherent energy. Heart-centered feelings like love and compassion expand heart energy to flourish in a stable, coherent flow.

Energetically, the heart is the master center for compassion, forgiveness, and, of course, love. When we experience these states, we are bathing in the heart's pure energy. Conversely, when we desire to amplify our feelings of love, compassion, or forgiveness, we can consciously bring our awareness to the heart space. This focused attention strengthens the heart's energy and helps us to connect more deeply with those loving expressions of ourselves.

We can strengthen certain qualities within us that will help us have a more open and expansive heart, allowing us to find that inner pathway to higher consciousness with greater ease. Consciously and intentionally bringing these qualities to the forefront of our living experience results in them naturally becoming our operating default state. Through our awareness and intentionality, we are able to re-pattern ourselves and strengthen the attributes we desire to embody.

Key qualities to focus on to open and expand the heart field include the following:

- **Love** - Being in a loving state naturally keeps the heart open. When we tune into the love that we feel, the energies of the heart are strong and radiant.

- **Compassion** - Understanding and accepting another regardless of their perceived flaws encourages the flow of heart energy in our being. Putting ourselves in another's shoes to understand their perspective opens the door to compassion.

- **Forgiveness** - Releasing another for the wrongs they have done unto us is essential to allowing the heart's energy to dominate our presence. Forgiving another does wonderful things to our own energy fields.

- **Acceptance** - Being in a state of acceptance allows us to just say *yes* to what life brings us. Acceptance is an allowing, open state of constantly changing flow. Through acceptance we trust that even the challenges we experience are for the highest good.

- **Gratitude** - As discussed in the section on journaling, being grateful attracts more into our lives for which to be grateful. Swimming in the warm waters of gratitude ignites a heart activation. Gratitude lights up the heart field.

Conversely, we may have filters in how we see ourselves and others that limit our heart's ability to flourish with the energies of love, compassion, forgiveness, acceptance, and gratitude. These filters keep the portal to the heart hidden. Here are some that are the most restrictive to the flow of heart energies.

- **Resentment** - We cannot be free until we release others from what they have done to us. It is often said that holding onto anger is like swallowing poison and expecting the other person to suffer. While our hope may be to punish another with our grudge, it is *our* energy that contracts and stifles. By holding the resentment, we stay outside the current of love. The person we are angry with may not even notice or care that we are directing our anger toward them. Ultimately, it's their choice whether to accept our perspective and take any responsibility for their role in our suffering. Only we can decide when we are finished blaming someone else for the way we feel.

- **Judgment** – Notice your inner critic. Unless we are in a rare, mystical state, we have a limited frame of reference about any given situation. We are privy to a little slice of the totality of a story based on our perspective. We must remember we have a peephole view before casting judgment. We are simply unable to fully understand another's motivation or perspective. Be mindful of self-criticism. Most people are their own harshest critics, but to what end? By constantly focusing on our flaws, we are not seeing the complete picture of the magnificence of the eternal being that we are. We are here to learn and grow! Along the way, stumbles and learnings are natural. Moving through life with no errors or things we wish we'd done differently might indicate living too much in our comfort zone with no attempts to expand.

- **Fear** - Love and fear exist on opposite ends of the spectrum. If we want to operate in a place of love, we must release ourselves from fear. Fear locks us into a place where we are seeking security. In seeking protection, we build walls around ourselves, which actually keep us isolated and disconnected. Love is open and trusting, and while that may make us feel vulnerable, nothing is stronger or truer than the energy of love. Love is the fabric of energy upon which this Universe is created. Nothing is braver or safer than standing open in the stream of love.

Resentment, judgment, and fear are tentacles that close around our heart field and keep it contracted, obscuring the path to higher consciousness. Energetically, they close us up and repel new possibilities from the Universe. Our energy fields just say *No*, and the insights, lessons, and opportunities that want to present to us instead just bounce off and cannot be received.

Refine Your Listening to the Heart

A stable, rhythmic, steady heart field that nurtures intuitive listening and knowing requires calmness and openness. To achieve a strong and cohesive heart energy field, it is essential to come into a place of calm centeredness.

There are several ways we can induce a state of calmness:

- Meditation

- Slow breathing, extending the exhale longer than the inhale

- Visualizing a peaceful meadow or lapping waves on a beach

- Intending calmness

- Bringing all of your awareness to the safety of this exact present moment

- Stepping barefoot outside on the earth and breathing deeply, or placing your hands on the earth for a few intentional breaths

To attune to the sensations of the heart and become more familiar with the inner workings of this hidden portal, close your eyes and think of someone or something that you really love. Drop your awareness down into your heart and simply notice how you feel. You may feel a warmth, a lift, a feeling of openness, or a swelling. You may sense or see with your inner sight a glow or light or notice another pleasant change. Allow your attention to strengthen these signals within your heart field. With practice, you can use these communication signals in real-time to gauge the state of your heart field, such as whether the heart feels expanded or contracted. Recognizing your heart's communication style allows you to receive its guidance and make adjustments in the moment.

Even if you don't feel particularly sensitive to feeling energy, you can refine your ability to understand the heart's messages through the simple practice offered at the end of this chapter.

Once you become familiar with your heart's communication, you can feel it, prompting you to notice its messages. I enjoy it when my heart feels warm and open for no particular reason. Instead of deliberately deciding to tune into my heart, it's as though the heart's own intelligence is giving me a little nudge: *Hey, check me out!* Then, my conscious awareness catches up to this radiant energy that has been pouring from my heart space.

Tuning into your heart space is an instrumental part of awakening and a key aspect of discovering this inner portal to higher consciousness. Live from your heart and be intentional about amplifying its field so you can unlock higher aspects of yourself.

Practice tuning into the communication system of your heart.

- Close your eyes and take a few cleansing breaths in through the nose and out through the mouth.

- Recall someone or something that you really love.

- Move your attention to the center of your chest and notice how you feel. Just observe without expectation.

- Notice any sensations, such as a change in temperature, a rush of tingles/chills, or a rising or opening/ blossoming sensation.

- If you're more of a visual person, you may see some light behind your closed eyes while your attention is in your heart center.

- If you naturally are more attuned to sound, perhaps a ringing tone will come to your attention.

- Write down your observations.

Repeat the practice over the next few days. Notice if you are consistently getting similar feedback from your heart as you continue connecting to it. You may notice one dominant sense that is easiest to perceive for your heart response.

Refine your ability to understand the heart's messages.

- Quiet your mind and take some deep breaths.

- Bring your awareness into your heart space, right in the center of your chest.

- *Feel* a yes. If you have no idea how to do that, simply imagine that you know how to feel a yes. Tell yourself, *If I knew what it was like to feel a yes, it would be like this.* Simply be aware of what your heart/the energy in the middle of your chest feels like. Don't *try.* Just let go of your expectations and notice what you feel.

- Keep your awareness in that same area, and now *feel* a no. Think to yourself, *If I knew what it was like to feel a no, it would be like this.* Notice if you feel or sense any difference in your heart space.

Don't overthink it or try too hard. Just play and explore. Let your body guide you and simply observe its response. The feelings can be subtle, particularly if you haven't tried to feel your energy before. Be patient and curious. The more you practice and pay attention to your body's response, the easier you will be able to recognize when your heart is giving you a yes or no in the moment when you need it most.

CHAPTER 8

REACHING NEW HEIGHTS

The first time I experienced an awareness of my soul as independent from my body was a premium event that blew the doors off my perceived limitations of the human experience.

About a year after I started a consistent meditation practice, I had a profound experience during one of my daily sessions. I felt my soul consciousness lifting, expanding beyond the confines of my body. I was sitting in my meditation posture, drawing all of my awareness —what I was focusing on—single-pointedly to the space between my eyebrows, where I could feel it connecting with the energy of my third-eye chakra. When my awareness, or focus, gathered into this powerful point, I felt my soul consciousness rising and lifting upwards. My body remained seated, and I was still aware of being inside it. But I also felt the boundaries of my body expanding beyond the physical. I was accessing places higher up in my awareness than before. It was as though I had been living in an apartment my whole life, and suddenly, the whole building was my home. I'd never been beyond the lower floors before, and through this experience, I suddenly found myself in an attic I hadn't known existed.

As this rising sensation of my soul consciousness progressed, I applied focus and concentration to stay with the experience and encourage its upward movement. I knew that if I broke my concentration, my awareness would return to body consciousness. Eventually, the lifting feeling ended and gave way to the sensation of being perched on an elevated platform with a 360-degree view.

This *view* from my perch was perceived with more of a felt sense than visually, although I could perceive that the entire scene around me was filled with radiant light. I enjoyed it immensely. Once the rising sensation stopped, I could relax the sustained focus I used to reach the platform. Reflecting upon the experience, an analogy of scaling a wall came to mind. Reaching the top may take a concentrated effort, but once there, it's effortless to relax and take in the view.

Until I reached the summit of that perch above my body, I had to apply intense, focused effort to ascend levels of consciousness until I broke a barrier and attained new heights of awareness where I could relax and enjoy the view, seen and unseen.

THIRD EYE OPENING

When I had that first consciousness-expanding experience, I was still rather green in understanding how energy and consciousness work in the human being. This peculiar sensation of rising and perching on an elevated platform, knowing perfectly well that my body was seated right where I had started my meditation, was perplexing. I had this same experience in a few subsequent meditations, but then it stopped. Looking back on this experience with the spiritual knowledge and understanding I've acquired since then, I now know it was an activation connecting my third eye and crown chakras for my psychic growth and expansion.

The third-eye, or sixth, chakra is an energy center generally thought to be located between the brain's left and right hemispheres at the mid-point between the eyebrows, slightly above the bridge of the nose. The crown, or seventh, chakra, also an energy center, is located at the top of the head. These two chakras are believed to relate to our psychic powers, giving us access to higher consciousness. The sensation of reaching a higher platform represented an expansion of my awareness to a soul-level consciousness reached through connecting these two chakras.

Completing the connection of my sixth and seventh chakras was a gradual process for me, happening spontaneously over a series of meditations. However, once the connection was fully online, that particular lifting experience in meditation ceased. As I became more familiar with accessing my soul consciousness, I didn't have to make the same effort to engage these chakra centers until, eventually, I didn't have a specific awareness of engaging them when I connected with higher consciousness.

In healing sessions, I have perceived clients experiencing similar chakra activations when they were on the verge of reaching new levels of their consciousness. Energetically, this felt like they were flickering in and out of two different levels of consciousness, rapidly and repeatedly expanding into a higher frequency and contracting back into a lower one. I had experienced this same oscillation between frequencies within myself when my heart chakra was shifting to a higher frequency, causing a palpable squeezing sensation in my chest. This perception of my clients' energies oscillating between two frequencies reflects the same process that caused the squeezing sensation in my chest. Eventually, they would be able to hold the higher frequency without oscillation, activating the affected chakra and bringing a new level of consciousness online.

THE SHIFT EXPERIENCE

Experiencing spiritual or personal growth is often described as a *shift* from one state of being to another. When we experience a shift in consciousness through meditation, it creates an inner change, moving us from one state of being or awareness to a new one. States of being are closely intertwined with our level of consciousness. For instance, finding ourselves often in a state of fear, anger, or focused on lack indicates we are operating on a lower level of consciousness. If we experience a shift to a higher level of consciousness, our state of being shifts to one of acceptance, joy, and abundance.

The pivotal work of Dr. David R. Hawkins, author of *Power vs. Force,* was groundbreaking in explaining the levels of consciousness.[20] Dr. Hawkins developed a scale of consciousness based on a person's primary vibrational frequency. Dr. Hawkins created a graphic depiction of this concept called the *Map of Consciousness*, which shows different states of being, defined as levels of consciousness, and their vibrational frequency measured on a relative scale of 1-1,000. According to Dr. Hawkins, shame is the lowest level of consciousness, with a numerical value of 20. Moving up the scale, anger, as a level of consciousness and frequency, has a numerical value of 150. Neutrality comes in at 250, acceptance at 350, and love is in the middle of the scale at 500. Levels of consciousness corresponding to enlightenment top the scale with a range of 700-1000.[21] While just this cursory measurement of levels of consciousness is revealing, a more comprehensive dive into Hawkins' work is an essential resource for a deeper understanding of the nature of the levels of human consciousness and how they relate to our behaviors and vibrations.

When we experience shifts in consciousness, we move up the scale of consciousness and operate from a different perspective. Over the course of life, our consciousness adapts to our age and accrued experience. We understand things differently at age 70 than we do at age 7. However, shifts in consciousness occur much more rapidly through deliberate soul development and alignment than by racking up birthday candles.

A consciousness shift experience may be subtle and gradual or quick and dramatic. Perhaps you've been meditating for a few months, and while you may not have had a lightning-bolt moment of realization in meditation, your state of being has changed over time. Perhaps you became more patient, deliberate, not so impulsive, calmer, happier, and less anxious than before you cultivated a meditation practice. Those qualities didn't appear overnight but came more and more to the forefront of your life experience as your consciousness shifted.

An all-at-once shift I witnessed occurred in a group meditation I guided where we were creating an energetic healing space and putting our loved ones in it. A participant shared afterward that she felt the healing energy in a more tangible way than she ever had in decades of meditation experience, so much so that her hands were actually vibrating throughout the meditation. In the space of just one meditation session, she had shifted to an entirely new level of sensory consciousness.

Shifts can also be momentary or lasting. Going back to the wall analogy, you may be able to leap up and catch a brief glimpse of what's on the other side before gravity pulls you back down. But if you climb the wall and sit at its ledge, you have a more complete view of the world beyond. Like the brief glimpse, a brief experience of a shift in consciousness can set the stage for a more profound shift, but dedicated focus and intention may be needed for lasting change.

Shifts also vary by individual. Someone who is not very self-aware may have a profound shift in consciousness from realizing more deeply how their actions affect others. The pleasure they derive from controlling others may dissolve and be replaced with a new and more gratifying appreciation for allowing people space to be their authentic selves. A shift can also look like being unable to forgive someone for years, then suddenly understanding, accepting, and forgiving their actions. Releasing the chains of anger and resentment shifts us to a lighter, higher-frequency version of ourselves. Other shifts, like the one experienced by the meditation participant, may open our psychic abilities to experience the visible perception of auras, the flow of energy, or a palpable connection to Source.

These energetic shifts can affect your whole being—body, mind, emotions, and soul. They may lead to a better intellectual understanding of esoteric concepts, but they are often beyond the rational mind and instead engage our feeling nature. You may know that a shift has happened in your life but be hard-pressed to express what it is like for you. The ability for others to understand and accept your inner experience has nothing to do with the validity of your experience.

Embrace Your Reality

External reality is experienced from the inside out. There is not one objective external reality that we are simply witnessing. Our experience of reality is subjective and inseparable from our *perception* of what is happening. Our perception of reality is inextricably linked to our level of consciousness. Our inner reality is informed by our level of consciousness and colors our unique experience of the outer world.

Shifts in our level of consciousness change our perception of our external reality, so realizing that we are not all experiencing the same reality is important. Collectively, we have a shared physical reality, but individually, we perceive that shared reality from vastly different perspectives. There are as many perceptions and experiences of that shared reality as there are individuals. How reality differs based on our unique perspectives also applies to many layers of our human experience, from the very practical to the less obvious.

A practical way that realities differ is simply through exposure. Your reality is different from mine because you have spent time doing and learning things that I have not, and vice versa.

For instance, lawyers spend many years attending law school, working in a law office, arguing in court, and meeting with clients. They are trained to consider what could go wrong to mitigate the risks and dangers of litigation. Their reality consists of knowing details about the law and legal system that don't even enter my awareness.

People born in China know Mandarin and what the air in their hometown smells like. They celebrate Chinese holidays, have longstanding family traditions I have never heard of, and eat food I've never seen on a menu.

Musicians have spent endless hours learning their craft. They know about tempo, how much breath to use to bring out the right note, and how to harmonize their voice or instrument. They may feel part of a current of music as if it is being played *through* them rather than *by* them. When they hear music, they hear more than the song and have opinions about the details of the composition that escape my attention. In my reality, music simply exists, and I only know whether I enjoy it or not.

But what if you and I are witnessing the same thing simultaneously, like going to a football game together? Does sharing the same external reality mean we'll have the same experience? Yes, we'll be in the same location at the same time, maybe even sitting next to each other, sharing the same view. But our inner reality may be vastly different depending on individual circumstances, preferences, perceptions, biases, and any number of other filters that make our experiences of reality entirely unique to each of us.

Sickeningly Fantastic Playoff Game

A great example of two very different experiences of the same event is when my husband and I went to the legendary Indianapolis Colts vs. New England Patriots playoff game for the 2006 AFC Championship. It was an important game not only for determining which team would go to the Super Bowl but also because Peyton Manning and Tom Brady were arguably the best quarterbacks of the time.

The first half was a disaster for the Colts; they were down 21-3 at halftime. Then, the Colts had an incredible second-half comeback and tied the game. The Patriots went ahead by three points with four minutes left in the fourth quarter, and in a very tense and exciting finish, the Colts managed to drive down 80 yards to score a touchdown and win the game.

What a spectacular game . . . for my husband. In those final minutes, as Peyton and the Colts were feverishly working their way to the end zone for the winning touchdown, my husband was on his feet, cheering at the top of his lungs right along with the rest of the stadium, watching sports history unfold in front of his eyes. I was feeling the thrill of the game, but I was also extremely nauseous. Between catching brief glimpses of history-in-the-making on the Jumbotron, I was staring at my shoes, breathing deeply, and desperately convincing myself not to throw up. I was in my first trimester of pregnancy with our first child, and my body hadn't received the instruction manual about how to confine morning sickness to the morning.

It wasn't just me and my husband whose inner realities were vastly different; Patriots fans who had traveled from Boston and elsewhere also had a very different experience of reality than ours. We witnessed one of the most important and incredible comebacks in the team's history while Patriots fans watched their team's 18-point lead fall apart. What Colts fans experienced as a miracle finish, Patriots fans experienced as a nightmare loss.

And while we spectators experienced our inner realities as fans of one team or the other, there were other realities for people whose jobs it is to play and coach those games. Livelihoods, along with personal pride and embarrassment, are at stake with such high-profile games. Even though part of a fan's reality may include some idealization about the dream jobs of the coaches, players, and other game insiders on the field and in the stands, playoff games are high-pressure career make-and-break moments. Again, they are in the same game at the same time but have a very different inner reality from the watching fans.

Bridging Divergent Inner Realities

Differences in our realities extend beyond the physical realm into levels of consciousness. As we develop spiritually, experience inward shifts, and access higher levels of awareness, we understand things in ways we've never considered before. We overcome our limiting beliefs, think new thoughts in new ways, experience life in ways we hadn't thought possible, and accept things we used to judge.

Our level of consciousness colors every encounter, causing us to see the world differently than others operating in another level of consciousness. As we continue to open up and become aware of higher truths, we will still encounter people operating from a narrower perspective that may be reminiscent of our previous view of reality. Our personal evolution does not mean everyone is likewise working on their growth or open to new ideas. After all, some people get older and wiser, and others just get older.

One way we bridge differing realities from our own is by finding common ground in a shared physical reality. However, navigating contradictory views of inner realities based on differing levels of awareness or consciousness can get tricky. Consider a thunderstorm. For some attuned to a survivalist level of consciousness, a fierce thunderstorm may be viewed only as threatening to persons or property. Others, who are more attuned to a planetary, environmentalist level of awareness, might view the storm as clearing the atmosphere and providing replenishing waters. Someone such as a shaman, attuned to a level of consciousness sensitive to energy and symbolism, might consider the storm's severity as a symbol or harbinger of intense energetic influxes raining down on Earth.

We can more easily express compassion and acceptance for those we travel through life with and encounter along the way when we remember that although we have common ground in the same physical event, we experience it differently through our subjective inner realities.

But what if there is no shared physical reality on which to find some common ground, like the existence of extraterrestrials?

My Shifting Inner Reality

There was a period in my life where I questioned the mental stability of those who believed in extraterrestrials.

In my youth, I was always intrigued by the idea of ETs living among the stars. As a child, it was one of my curiosities about the world, but adulthood introduced me to many people I respected and considered intelligent who disregarded the notion of life beyond Earth. I eventually discounted my childhood curiosity as fantasy and became convinced that aliens were not real and that believing in such things was silly. Later, as my spiritual exploration deepened, I slowly opened again to the possibility of life outside of Earth, ultimately becoming very accepting and knowledgeable on the subject of extraterrestrials and welcoming many experiencers and UFO researchers on my podcast. Now, it is one of my favorite topics to explore; finding people to share stories and theories about life beyond this planet lights me up. I feel a kinship with those who are also drawn to the subject of ETs despite any lingering social stigmas projected by the masses.

If I had talked about ETs with someone who insisted they were real when I thought it was a silly proposition, the conversation wouldn't have gone far. According to my reality at that time, aliens didn't exist, and I shouldn't put much stock into anyone trying to convince me otherwise. ET encounters just didn't fit into my box of what was possible. My contracted view of reality didn't have room for that possibility, so it would have been hard for me to have a fruitful conversation with an ET experiencer or someone who was ET-curious at that time.

Since then, I have accumulated hours of time diving into extremely convincing stories and purported cover-ups. I've seen unexplainable things in the sky and had inner experiences with otherworldly beings. But I cannot expect someone who has not accepted the possibility of life beyond this planet to take my word that ETs exist. I have also had their perception of reality and understand wanting to protect oneself from looking silly and naïve based on what authority figures in the media and government say is untrue. It took years of exposure to a different view than mine to shift my inner reality to accept the likely existence of ETs—again.

Compassion for Differing Perspectives

Evolving and expanding consciousness changes how we respond to repeated triggers that show up in our lives. As consciousness expands and we access higher levels of awareness, so does our understanding and acceptance expand.

We can choose to remember when our box was smaller and recognize when someone else is still confined to a smaller box. When we were operating from a lower level of consciousness—a narrower perspective that was perhaps locked into a survival or lack mentality —our thoughts, words, and actions were different than when we expanded into a higher, more loving perspective. We can give others grace when their actions don't line up with how we want them to think and act. We remember and trust that there is a divine timing to all things, and the journey for that person to awaken to their soul and embody a higher level of consciousness will happen in its own way and in due time.

Employing humility is crucial as you navigate the challenges that arise from humanity existing across a wide spectrum of consciousness. As far as we may have come in our own understanding through raising our vibration, the human mind is still very limited in its ability to fathom the complexity and vastness of the Universe. Personally, each mystical experience and expansion of consciousness that presents new understandings to me is accompanied by more mystery that I can't completely wrap my head around.

When interacting with someone with a perspective that repels us, keeping our hearts open and finding compassion is crucial. We may not be able to relate to their way of thinking — and they may not be ready to understand our perspective—but when we truly embody our Higher Self, we can choose to hold them in our hearts despite the mismatch of vibrational frequency. They may eventually see our perspective as they continue their spiritual evolution, or, in a twist that I would not put past this clever Universe, our own evolution may reveal truths currently hidden from us, making us understand their repulsive perspective in a new light.

Our personal reality is born from our experience, which has been heavily influenced by who raised us, the culture we were brought up in, the media we have plugged ourselves into, our schooling, and so forth. It's helpful to keep in mind the differing opportunities and experiences that may have led us to another level of consciousness than someone else. We don't know the circumstances surrounding the level of programming and the sources of influence another has been up against in the course of their life.

Neale Donald Walsch addresses this masterfully in his book, *The God Solution*, which we discussed when he was a guest on my podcast.[22] Surprisingly, he said that at a certain point on the spiritual journey, forgiveness actually impedes spiritual growth. What he is suggesting is that while forgiveness is important for opening the heart, it's possible to, in a sense, graduate out of it. Forgiveness implies letting someone off the hook for the wrong they have done. A higher version of forgiveness, however, is compassionate acceptance.

When we can truly come to acceptance, we have a more complete view of another's actions and perspective. We honor where they are on their path, understand the level of consciousness that led to their actions, and accept the seeming missteps that negatively impact us. Like us, they are a spirit having a complicated human experience, and mistakes are fertile ground for growth. We don't even have the full picture of our own spiritual path, let alone anyone else's path, no matter how spiritually evolved we believe ourselves to be. Remembering our own meandering path with its many foibles helps us to extend grace to others, giving them the benefit of the doubt and advancing our spiritual growth.

Self-Compassion

Being in acceptance does not mean subjecting ourselves to poisonous friendships or romances when it is clear they are detrimental to our happiness and soul growth. Accepting that someone who has placed us in the crosshairs of their anger is acting out of a lower level of consciousness does not mean being a doormat for their hurtful behavior. Instead, that acceptance is tempered with self-compassion. Compassionate acceptance of others also means respecting our own needs as paramount and mitigating the harmful situation to prevent further harm from internalizing grudges, heartache, and anger toward the other person.

If we confuse compassionate acceptance with permitting ourselves to be mistreated, we send a message that mistreatment is acceptable. We owe it to ourselves and those harming us to break cycles of toxic relationships. Allowing someone to drag us into a lower vibration through their abuse, anger, or condescension reinforces that lower level of consciousness within them, enabling their abusive tendencies. But by disentangling ourselves from their lower frequency energy, we remove ourselves as a target for playing the role of victim to the abuser. Upholding healthy boundaries by refusing to remain caught up in an unhealthy dynamic invites the other person to release their low vibrational patterns and enter a new level of consciousness if they are ready and willing.

Recognizing that someone is continuously knocking us down or holding us back and having the courage to break the pattern is essential for spiritual growth. Through this act of self-compassion, we expand our consciousness and create a wake where people can experience a higher reality. Whether we are decisively modeling healthy boundaries or simply reflecting a higher frequency version of reality, energetically, we open new levels of possibility for everyone we meet and even those we don't.

Expansion into Unknown Territories of Consciousness

One of my greatest pleasures is experiencing my external sensory perception giving way to my inner awareness of a multidimensional experience. I feel deep fulfillment when my inner sight awakens, bringing other realms and dimensions into view. But there can be a bit of Wild West unruliness to what appears. It's not always angel choirs and crystalline roses. Sometimes, more shadowy figures come to the forefront.

The more my consciousness has expanded, and these other realms have come more fully into my awareness, the more important it has become to manage my fear. In a multidimensional—or quantum—experience, the vibrational state of being is a big factor in determining the experience. Some encounters can be scary at first, causing me to drop into a lower frequency of fear that can spiral. Occasionally, I have seen shapes and forms with my mind's eye that looked reptilian or demonic. Honestly, when they first came into focus, it was alarming! My initial reaction is to worry that I've gotten myself into trouble on the astral plane. I feel vulnerable and don't want to be overpowered by any such dark entity.

My defense is to find and hold a state of neutrality, which allows the unpleasant visions to come and go without me becoming attached to them and spiraling into a state of fear. While I cannot control what images appear during my multidimensional journeys, I *am* in control of how I feel about what appears. I can buy into something being scary, or I can stand in my power and decide that what I am seeing with my inner eye is only scary if I choose that perception of my inner reality.

I find it immensely helpful to challenge my initial fear-based thoughts about these dark encounters with curiosity and the possibility that what is appearing before me is ultimately for my growth. When I shift from fear to neutrality, I immediately transform what appeared to be a potential psychic threat into a powerful lesson in my courage and inner power. Questions will flash through my mind as I look for the key to unlocking the mystery of transforming my fear.

- Am I seeing this to test my resolve for not easily succumbing to fear?

- Is my Higher Self in disguise teaching me that I have nothing to be afraid of?

- Am I seeing representations of shadow aspects of myself that I have not wanted to acknowledge?

- Is this an opportunity to face these shadows, helping me to release them?

- How much light can I know and hold if I am never confronted by darkness?

- Can I remember the immense light I am when looking at fiery eyes and menacing teeth right inside my own inner realm?

- Can I hold my divine power when faced with a predatory figure?

- Could it even be that I am seeing a fierce guardian, such as a dragon, who is actually protecting me?

Examining fearful thoughts to unleash their transformative power alchemizes fear into a spiritual gift for expanding consciousness. By providing an impetus to connect with the higher-frequency consciousness needed to overcome and release the grip of fear, it serves as an important catalyst on our spiritual journey. Attaching to fear and allowing it to pervade our thoughts propels us into lower frequencies, making us vulnerable to negative influences and experiences in both the outer and inner worlds. However, in the same way that attaching to fear takes us spiraling downward in a self-perpetuating cycle of more fear, releasing it shifts the direction of our thoughts, spiraling them upward in a self-perpetuating cycle of neutrality that grows into acceptance and ultimately to the frequency of love, which cannot be penetrated by lower-frequency energy or consciousness.

I had an insightful conversation with my friend Sam that made me consider the deeper implications of fear in our human experience. He is a psychiatrist trained in a Western medical view of the mind but is interested in my mystical psychic experiences. In our conversation, I was describing the visual and sensory aspects of my experiences, and Sam wanted to know more. He started asking more probing questions about how the experiences made me feel and the value I get from them. I thought about it and said they give me a broader understanding of life, revealing that our daily worries don't matter the way we think they do. Not satisfied, Sam pressed on, asking me *why* that was my response. That prompted me to give another response followed by another *why*. We went on like this until we finally realized that, ultimately, my multidimensional experiences had revealed the existence of my soul beyond human reality to such an extent that I no longer feared death. It was an epiphany for us both.

On reflection, I could see how experiencing my consciousness beyond a human form had transformed my view of mortality. Having glimpsed reality beyond this human experience, I have, to some extent, seen what awaits me after I release this human body through the death process, leaving me certain that death is the soul's transition from one state of existence to another. Death is not *the end*, just *an end* followed by a new beginning. Releasing my fear of death and awakening to a perspective that life is so much more than our physical experience has been deeply transformative.

I believe the grand purpose underlying all human life is to expand the sense of self beyond the physical and bring more of our spiritual light and gifts into our being. Being caught up in the lower vibrational hold of fear is incongruent with our expansion, light, and gifts. The more we are in fear, the more we close up and hold back. But we are strong. We have everything we need to recognize and overcome the fear game.

Let go of fear! When it arises, transform it with love, acceptance, and neutrality.

_do it!_

Think about your perceived reality as it is right now. Take out your journal and write your reflections to the following prompts.

- Bring to mind a difficult situation you are in or have recently experienced with another person. Take time to think through and feel into what that experience was like for you. Remember the actions that caused the feelings you had. Recall any confusion you experienced relating to the words or actions of the other person and the judgments it created within you. Write them down in your journal.

- Now, put yourself in the perspective of the other party. Do your best to look at the same issue you have just been writing about, but from their perspective. Think about life from their perspective. Imagine how their life experience has shaped them from the time they were a child, which would make them experience the situation the way they did and create the reaction within them that it did. Can you stay in their perspective long enough to gain some understanding of how they interpreted the situation in the way they did, which caused the challenge between you? Be as open and honest as possible to experience their version of reality. Come into neutrality and simply witness the situation as an observer, without the charge that comes from viewing it only from your perspective. Capture your reflections from this perspective in your journal.

• Allow your perception of the challenge from both your perspective and theirs to bring forgiveness and healing into this situation. From this place of neutrality, consider if this situation stems from a toxic pattern between you and the other person. Be honest with yourself about whether new, clearer boundaries are necessary through this experience.

CHAPTER 9

THE SLIPPERY SLOPE OF CULTS

Yes, it's time to talk about cults.

In modern times, there is a tendency for self-proclaimed spiritual leaders to position themselves as gurus for the purpose of seeking idolization over reverence. While true gurus have indeed graced this Earth many times, many others have embraced spiritual leadership for power and personal gain. Woven into their messages of spiritual truths are reprimands and ritual practices exerting control over their followers, diminishing rather than uplifting the Divine within.

The spiritual path is littered with these self-serving *leaders* who had cultivated a following so devout in their worship that a cult, or cult-like community, forms around them, drawing in more followers like moths to a flame. Being mindful of the slippery slope from seeking spiritual growth to being caught in a web of spiritual superiority, manipulation, and self-serving agendas is a uniquely transformative lesson on the awakening path that many have encountered in some manner.

WOLVES IN SHEEP'S CLOTHING

Cults can be very tricky territory because the leaders and their devout followers are well-disguised wolves in sheep's clothing. The enticing displays of inner power and spiritual realization are easily confused with true mastery. While cult members and their leaders present an outward appearance of profound transformative powers and divine awakening that makes them an attractive lure to the unsuspecting, beneath the surface is a corrupt underbelly of power, control, and egoic agendas driven by lies and misdirection.

The cult's self-proclaimed secret recipe for enlightenment comes with the requirements of a strong commitment to follow the chosen methods and teachings and increasing amounts of time, attention, and, of course, money to reach some ultimate level of inner enlightenment. Believing the propaganda and proclamations, followers trustingly divest their personal power, submitting entirely to the prescribed regimen of worship and ritual, believing they have found a true path to enlightenment.

No cult is worth its salt without a charismatic and compelling *guru* who displays godlike psychic powers, healing abilities, physical manifestations seemingly out of thin air, and any number of other magical powers that reinforce the illusion of Divine appointment. But take away the fever pitch of cult devotion overflowing from adoring followers, and the underlying wolf is revealed. What would otherwise be a commonplace display of natural psychic abilities is catapulted to a divine superpower under the spellbinding charisma of the cult leader. Worse is the intentional use of illusion, magic trickery, or even black magic to herald dark forces for conjuring delusional states of awareness, making followers supremely vulnerable to their time and finances being siphoned on the false promise that a path to heaven or ascension will be paved by more time, energy, and money going to the cult.

Cults and cult leaders are nothing new in human history, so they have a well-proven track record of telltale signs that followers have fallen for a false guru. Here are some common signs of cult devotion taking a turn for the worse:

- Giving an incredible amount of money, under the guru's advice that the donation will finance God's work, and the support will be karmically rewarded as money or spiritual gifts in this lifetime or another.

- Spending time and energy evangelizing the guru's teachings to recruit followers, believing that only those who are privy to the teachings will be spared when some near-future catastrophe predicted by the guru happens in this life or the afterlife and, thus, wanting to save others from a terrible fate. In truth, these new followers are being funneled into the cult to increase the money and power flowing to the guru without the guru needing to put forth personal effort into recruiting.

- Severing ties with family and friends, believing the guru's admonition that this is required to keep a high vibration and not get distracted from the path to enlightenment. The admonition is merely a guise for idolizing the guru and giving the cult greater control over followers by eliminating outside voices of reason that conflict with grooming within the organization.

- Allowing the guru to be the liaison between God and oneself out of a belief that the most direct path to God is through the guru. Followers believe that a certain spiritual level, which they do not have, must be attained to be worthy of a personal relationship with God when, in truth, God is available to everyone. This wedge prevents them from developing their own meaningful relationship with God, which would render the guru's influence and teachings unnecessary.

- Believing the guru's teachings to be the one true or fastest path to enlightenment. Followers believe the guru is *the* divinely chosen savior, and they feel special for recognizing this embodied Divine being and their special role for humanity.

- Shutting out and rejecting all other spiritual teachings from others so as not to *become confused.* Similar to severing ties with family and friends, this gives the guru more control over the follower. The spell is harder to break if no outside influences are challenging what the guru is saying. It also means that any plagiarism by the guru is less likely to be detected because the followers hear it from them first, even if it's been ripped off from other spiritual leaders.

- Being subjected to sexual misconduct by a superior within the cult under the pretense that this person can transfer Divine energy sexually. Sexual abuse is also used as a way to gain a follower's complete surrender, trust, or acceptance of the guru, teachings, and path. Engaging in such behavior demonstrates their surrender and devotion.

- Allowing the guru and cult rules to completely dominate daily life, from what and how much to eat, when and how long to sleep, how to spend time, who to interact with, and, in more extreme cases, the bathroom schedule.

As alarming and obvious as this list of terribles may seem for alerting someone to suspect *cult*, it's not that simple. You might think that with such behavior being well outside your normal operating mode, it would be easy to spot entanglement with a cult, and you will, thus, never find yourself in that situation. However, be forewarned that it can be tricky business discerning who truly desires to help you advance on your path and who is using spiritual truths to their own advantage at your expense. Before you find yourself in the more appalling situations listed above, well-planned groundwork to develop your trust and sense of community has been laid out to make you feel special and secure—not to mention vulnerable.

A SPOTTING IN THE WILD

My own skill at spotting a cult has been honed from experience. I wandered into this murky territory when something that initially appeared very special and divine eventually revealed itself as a cult.

I share a fictionalized version of my personal story with great love, trust, and a healthy dose of embarrassment for the sole purpose of illustrating just how easy it can be to slide from spiritual seeker to cult member. My aim in sharing my experience is to arm you with an inside perspective so you can sidestep the pitfalls of landing in a cult should you find yourself at the precipice of a slippery slide.

My cult story started with a serendipitous opportunity for an online meeting with the leaders of an organization claiming to offer powerful wisdom teachings for attaining enlightenment, which only they had been entrusted to share with humanity. Being of a curious nature, I was intrigued by this unexpected opportunity. Though my suspicions were heightened by anyone claiming to be solely endowed with the one true quick path to enlightenment, I had to pick up the proverbial breadcrumb and see where it led.

In preparation for our meeting, I did my research to find out what I could about these people and have at least some familiarity with their story, given they had graciously offered to spend some time with me. I was a bit surprised at the extent of their following and the depth of their teachings and offerings. At this point, I was fairly familiar with the mind-body-spirit landscape through my podcasts and research and hadn't yet heard of these people or the organization. I was also surprised at the cost of some of the programs and retreats they offered. The more I researched, the more red flags came up until I realized what was niggling at me—this had to be a cult. At first, I laughed off my *ah-ha* moment, and the thought of *Bonnie and Clyde* came to me, thinking of the shrewd scams and heists they pulled off as seemingly heroic characters.

I checked in with a few friends who all agreed on the telltale markings of a cult—charismatic leaders claiming to have the one and only true path to enlightenment, confusing language that only they could unpack to reveal the truth, and images of worshippers at their feet in states of bliss and awe. Oh, and don't forget the extravagant costs of being part of their world.

"Ok, good," I thought, "it's confirmed. This is a cult. Ignore it."

Yet even with this and everything inside of me screaming that these guys are fakes, what is life if not an adventure? I patted the red flags and warnings sweetly on the head as though they were beloved protective pets and allowed curiosity to get the better of me.

"It's ok, guys, I know what I'm doing," I said to those warnings with a wink.

The Wasps' Nest

So, there it was. I accepted the invitation to meet online. After all, it couldn't hurt to have a quick listen, right?

I mean, my guard is up; I'm hip to the game here. I'd be the last person to fall prey to cult leaders. It could actually be a little funny to see their pickup lines.

Fast forward to the meeting. Introductions were made, and admittedly, I was oddly star-struck by this Bonnie and Clyde team. The charm offensive was on full blast. I hadn't prepared for that. I quickly regained my composure and thanked them for this special opportunity to learn more about them and their teachings. By this point in my spiritual path, I was fairly familiar with a range of spiritual teachings and given my predisposition that this was nothing more than a cult scam, I did not expect to be moved by the conversation. But, again,

I was surprisingly taken aback by some of their comments and realized I was hearing some really provocative stuff.

"Ok, this is getting interesting," I thought. Maybe I had been too hasty in my judgment.

I could feel myself softening, thinking, "*Huh,* maybe Bonnie and Clyde are on to something here."

As I listened, I heard spiritual truths that I was already familiar with, along with new insights I hadn't heard before but fit into my understanding. They talked about ascension, going into a lot of technical details beyond theory and philosophy. The concepts they discussed that I already knew signaled that they were aligned with my spiritual knowing and fit into my existing paradigm; this provided a hook for their new intel about wisdom and knowledge that had so far evaded me. My curiosity was baited, and the gatekeepers of this new intel had drawn me to their door.

Of course, our meeting was just an introduction, and they could only share the more advanced knowledge they were privy to with students who were true followers with a level of dedication that most people aren't suited for. The most deeply sacred and secret teachings were certainly not appropriate to share with those not vetted to hold such wisdom.

Ok, I thought, I'm not like most people. I *am* deeply dedicated to my spiritual development. Maybe the knowledge and insights they offered are part of my path. I was not about to let such a unique opportunity for knowledge that had landed right in my lap pass me by. The inner dialogue ensued. What if the Universe was presenting exactly what I needed on a platter for a massive step in my development? Was I so arrogant that I would use my ego's biases to decide at a glance whether something was valuable? Sure, everything about them on the outside screamed *cult*, but perhaps those preconceived judgments they trigger just serve to separate the wheat from the chaff.

I felt oddly humbled by my conversation with Bonnie and Clyde. I shared some of my experience with the same friends who suspected this was a cult, and most of them agreed that they hadn't heard the concepts we discussed from anyone else. To put it lightly, we had a collective feeling of being a bit blown away by the insights shared by these cult leaders, Bonnie and Clyde. Like me, the others had come around to a dubious but compelling feeling that, indeed, these were special people to be taken seriously.

Thirsty for more, I sought out many of their online teachings and signed up for their retreat. I was taken aback by the price but justified it as an exceptional opportunity to be in the presence of such special people.

To *qualify* for their retreat, I had to take their signature course, which was also a hefty investment for an online course. I rationalized that my spiritual development was worth it. I also felt that by purchasing their courses, I was not only getting the value of new insights and expansion but also contributing to their mission of awakening humanity. The more funds they had, the greater their reach, which was better for everyone. It was a win-win-win, even if it was drying up my personal funds and sucking up my time and energy away from my own soul's mission to elevate humanity with my personal gifts. Incidentally, I had some help with these justifications as the idea of funding God's work was encouraged in several of their interviews and talks that I eagerly consumed.

If It Dresses Like a Duck . . .

Qualified and paid up, I attended the retreat.

I was so happy to be there. Still, at every stage of the retreat activities, a part of me evaluated what was happening, trying to ascertain the level of culty-ness. To my surprise, I wasn't the only one there with a skeptic on their shoulder, as the cult topic came up frequently among participants.

Chatter among small break-out groups went something like this: "Wow, these grounds are just divine . . . That satsang was so powerful . . . So, do you think this a cult?"

The exchange was followed by self-conscious laughter as we bantered about the things that seemed cultish, how this must look like a cult from the outside, then resolutely concluded this was definitely NOT a cult.

Still, there was a collective mannerism, dress, and language among the long-term followers, mid-level teachers, and organizational administrators that reeked of *cult*. I remember a palpable internal red flag warning that I may be wading in cult waters. But I was there for the promise of a profoundly transformative experience and kept my mind open.

Those who had been involved with this organization for much longer than me would talk about how the people in their lives just didn't get it. Friends and family would tell them these leaders were no good, but of course, being outside the organization, they weren't at the right frequency to understand. I shared my anecdote many times about how, at first glance, *even I* had marked them as cult leaders and dismissed them—silly, arrogant me.

Honestly, my experience at the retreat was mostly expansive, loving, and fulfilling. I loved connecting with so many others who were nurturing their spiritual lives and navigating modern living while prioritizing their spiritual growth. We felt unified in a shared purpose of advancing our own souls into a higher frequency and helping humanity enter a new stage of evolution, as we were led to believe. We reinforced within each other the belief that we were part of something profound and meaningful for ourselves and humanity through this organization.

Paradoxically, the retreat experience allowed me to witness with my own eyes the telltale warning signs of a cult while simultaneously solidifying the belief that the leaders possessed priceless ancient knowledge that could lead everyone to enlightenment. Throughout the retreat, they repeatedly assured us of their ability to steer people to everlasting life. In other words, they were convincing us that they held the keys to living in our human bodies forever, not dying, EVER. As much as my logical mind was at odds with this, it was a revolutionary proposition that excited me.

Throughout the retreat, my assessments of what I was experiencing oscillated tirelessly, from a profound and pivotal opportunity for spiritual growth to being hoodwinked. While many promises of grandiose spiritual development and a rapid evolutionary shift for humanity ushered in by the work of this organization seemed too good to be true, in the bubble of that retreat's environment, anything and everything seemed possible. I continuously grappled with internal questions about what I was participating in.

A cult wouldn't make me feel so good, right?

I wouldn't feel such love and appreciation for the leaders and fellow members if it wasn't for my highest good. Right?

Most importantly, I would *know* if this was a cult, right? It would be on the letterhead of the membership papers I signed in blood during the naked full moon ritual. There was none of that stuff, so it wasn't a cult. I was pretty sure, kind of.

Looking back, I have to laugh when I think about the retreat and how often conversation turned to how much this non-cult had the air of a cult, yet we joined together in some unspoken bond to convince ourselves of its legitimacy.

Doubling Down

Despite the warning signs, my enthusiasm and curiosity prevailed, and ultimately, the retreat experience prompted me to double down on my belief that the teachings and teachers were spectacular and legitimately transformative. I even had the teachers on my podcast and attested to my personal experience, growth, and benefits from the teachings. I also interviewed for an internal position to help them with their written copy and whatever other service I could offer.

As an aside, rest assured that both of my interviews about these teachings have long since been removed from my podcast feed, lest they entice anyone else to join.

Looking back, the real sticking point for me is that I was more than ready to funnel my valuable time, energy, and talent into serving a cultist agenda, buying into the idea that these people were the true bringers of light. I was convinced that my highest service would be to do whatever I could to strengthen their reach at the expense of the work I am here to do with my one wild and precious life.

At that point, I was fully entangled in the cult's web of illusion and delusion. Had I not woken up to the truth of what was happening, I could easily have watered down or given up completely on pursuing my own divine mission. Fortunately, my Higher Self had a say in writing the closing chapter of my cult story and led *Little Kara* out of her elaborately constructed trap.

THE ILLUSION DISSOLVES

Shortly after the retreat, the veil of illusion finally started to lift. I began to hear personal accounts from people who had been part of Bonnie and Clyde's inner circle that things were not as they appeared. There were alarming accounts of disconnects between what the leaders taught and how they lived, from what they claimed to eat to how they treated people. There were claims of organization leadership having frequent angry outbursts and not respecting boundaries for the basic needs of others, such as depriving them of sleep and rest breaks. Other claims underscored various ways in which leadership manipulated staff and followers through misinformation and misdirection.

As more gossip and stories emerged from followers, I heard about the organization allegedly receiving *huge* donations from members. The overall price tag for the retreat that I had considered shocking was mere pennies compared to what I heard about what others claimed to have contributed. There were also disturbing tales of possible fraudulent activity involving offshore accounts and other unethical behavior related to financial dealings.

Plagiarism was another issue. Some followers claimed that the organization had used their written or artistic work without seeking consent or giving them credit. I also witnessed an instance of plagiarism that I personally found shocking at the time. It happened when Clyde used a well-known quote from Paramahansa Yogananda at a teaching I attended. I immediately recognized the quote and waited for the appropriate credit to be given to Yogananda for his wise words. But there was none—nothing. Clyde just looked at us, beaming with arrogance and pride, while followers gazed back with big, goofy smiles in glassy-eyed innocence.

In the years since my cult experience, the continued pursuit of quenching my spiritual thirst has revealed that several of the purportedly *special and unique* teachings I first heard in my cult stint were actually the original works of others that pre-dated the formation of this organization. YouTube videos explaining the exact spiritual sciences that the cult leaders touted as their own include the original work of Dr. Joe Dispenza and Richard Rudd, author of the iconic work *The Gene Keys: Embracing Your Higher Purpose.*[23] Of course, strongly discouraging members from following any other spiritual teachings was a clever way to conceal such sources, giving self-proclaimed gurus ample room to wrap groundbreaking teachings from others in their own packaging and claim them as their own.

Just knowing these allegations had surfaced and that people in the organization were genuinely concerned was enough for me to suspect that an oppressive cult reality lay hidden behind a carefully curated illusion of divine grace and perfection.

Twisted Truths

In the wrong hands, spiritual truths can be twisted and used against you.

Someone can have keys to higher consciousness or spout spiritual truths, but that does not mean that they are actually embodying those truths or using them for the highest benefit of everyone. They may speak as though they are of the light and are high-frequency beings, but sometimes, it's just intellectual knowledge and not wisdom they have truly mastered. They can use high truths to lure followers, then manipulate those truths to raise themselves higher on the pedestal and hold down their followers. Add in a bit of charisma, and followers will be tripping over themselves to hand over their trust, power, and *money!*

Many people have access to divine truths from books, social media, online courses, live events, and more. So, it's not surprising that cult teachings are commonly copied from an established source to give them an air of familiarity that reinforces trust, speaking a language that resonates with their target followers. Setting aside the immorality and illegality of plagiarism, the real harm to cult followers is the twist—how the teaching is manipulated to serve the cult leader's agenda.

Take, for instance, the truth that there are different levels of consciousness. There is a plethora of teachings and information to support the idea that we operate within and emit a vibrational frequency corresponding to a level of consciousness. So, it rings true when cult leadership leans into this concept, isolating followers by claiming that outsiders don't share the same high-frequency consciousness and they or their teachings can't be trusted. Applying that same logic, followers who leave or question the cult's teachings and methods are shamed for having a lower level of consciousness than needed to understand the teachings.

Warning: Contents Under Pressure

A good test for determining if a purported spiritual leader is actually a cult leader wolf beneath the sheepskin of their finely curated public persona is how they react under pressure when not in the spotlight. It is very telling to witness a so-called spiritual leader who claims to be liberated from their ego throw angry tantrums or hurl insults at others over supposed transgressions from leaving the organization to normal human error or miscommunication.

An authentic spiritual master who has truly overcome lower egoic tendencies holds a higher perspective of doing no harm that transcends such negative and hurtful reactions. People who have attained true spiritual mastery and enlightenment are very rare and operate at the highest levels of compassion, empathy, and sensitivity toward others, in good times and in bad. The trust and warmth one would feel from engaging with such a truly enlightened being would be held as an unbreakable sacred bond and promise of their selfless service.

That's the slippery slope of cults. They feel so inclusive and welcoming until your eyes are opened to the cult leader's thinly veiled control and service-to-self agenda, creating an atmosphere of *us vs. them, in or out* to conceal hidden landmines just waiting to explode.

Liberation!

Eventually, I escorted myself out the door. My cult lesson was done. I learned and grew in some ways while under Bonnie and Clyde's enchantment, but when it no longer aligned with my spiritual path, I found the courage to walk away, grateful and relieved to have been roused from sleeping at the wheel.

Shortly after my group retreat experience, I noticed several people were leaving the organization, perhaps having seen it for the cult that it was. As I heard more accounts of suspicious behavior by the organization's leadership, I was eventually convinced that my initial suspicions of a cult following were correct. Perhaps for the lesson I needed to learn or just sheer curiosity, my mind overwrote those initial suspicions in the pursuit of advanced teachings.

Trekking on our personal spiritual paths is usually not a straight line. We may think we've found a new pathway when we're actually looping back and revisiting ground that has already been covered but has a new lesson or purpose. When I was a child, I went to a Christian church. I was content with churchgoing for many years until I began to see how Jesus was used by religion to control parishioners, and I stopped going to church. That experience left me feeling disconnected from Jesus for many years. Coming full circle, Jesus again has a very prominent role in my spirituality, but without the religious dogma.

Meeting Bonnie and Clyde with their brand of Jesus's teachings struck a chord going all the way back to my childhood about the powerful teachings of Jesus. I thought I found a new pathway, a shortcut for revealing the real truth of his teachings on the path to enlightenment. While that was not exactly how the path played out, and my cult experience didn't take me toward enlightenment as I had intended, it was not lost ground. In hindsight, I was able to see how my re-ignited connection to Jesus had brought me powerful, though unexpected, gifts.

The most important gift was the opportunity to choose myself! When the veil was lifted, and I had clear sight of the wolf that had been hiding in fleece, I remembered who I was and stepped back into myself.

I was shocked by the experiences shared by others. I was saddened that what I had hoped was so special was an illusion. I was angered by the sense of manipulation and siphoning of followers' money and energy. I was, frankly, embarrassed that I fell for it.

But as their theater set crashed down around me, an opportunity arose to reclaim myself. I knew the path to God was within me, and this detour was a wake-up call for me to step into my personal power. I recognized that I had handed over my power and authority in my enthusiasm for access to a perceived savior. I realized I would never truly come into my personal mastery with that mindset or behavior.

The Baby and the Bathwater

I have shared my experience to help you, and anyone you know who might benefit from my story, to understand how easy it is to journey down the slippery slope of cults, especially in these times of so much access to spiritual messages through social media. Flashy reels and posts promising quick enlightenment are certainly appealing to seekers. A big online following can draw us in. We might confuse a high like count for legitimate spiritual aptitude. It's important to employ our discernment and stay in alignment with our own Higher Self to help navigate the online community terrain.

If you find that you have slid down a cult slope, it might be natural to feel stupid and berate yourself for being gullible or for whatever else you want to tell yourself about how you got into that situation. That's OK. Feel those feelings *then let them go!* Don't miss the important second half of the previous sentence. Let yourself experience the emotions that come when the illusion crashes, but don't get stuck there. Move through those initial lower vibrational feelings and allow yourself to come out the other side of them.

This is your time to shine and step into your next level of sovereignty and self-mastery. Own your role in how curiosity led you to choices that landed you here. You *are* responsible for those choices and where they led—no blame, no shame, no guilt—just an honest acceptance of your power and what happens when you hand it over to others. The cult experience is a portal to lived wisdom through experience, and if you allow it, it can propel you to greater compassion, acceptance, and liberation.

Anyone finding themselves on their own cult journey must remember self-compassion. Cult leaders are very adept narcissistic predators who deliberately keep the wool pulled over your eyes as long as they can. Unfortunately, black magic is really a thing in this world, and that tactic could have even been used to keep you locked in without your knowledge or consent. Many people don't know how to come out from under a *spell*, and particularly, being in a vulnerable place with people we trust not only with our lives but also with the afterlife makes us especially susceptible to that energetic manipulation.

When coming out of a cult experience, be mindful of two knee-jerk reactions that could further muddy your path forward. First is jumping right into another spiritual organization. You might feel adrift after leaving a spiritual community and be naturally attracted to another group or leader very soon, similar to coming out of one toxic relationship only to jump into the arms of the next person you come across. In both cases, giving yourself the tender loving care, time, and space needed for healing so thoughts and feelings can settle until you return to your center is important.

The second reaction to watch out for is throwing out the baby with the bathwater. When you feel burned by a cult experience, you may be tempted to believe everything spiritual is false or dangerous. If parts of spiritual teachings were used against you, you may feel none of it is true or good for you. Remember that cults are notorious for taking the truth and manipulating it for their own gain. But the highest truths are universal and unchanging. Here are some universal truths that can guide you even in your darkest moments of doubt.

- You are an eternal spirit.

- You have guides on the other side.

- You have purpose.

- You are a divine being who is eternally loved.

- You are supported by a benevolent Universe.

Ultimately, I am grateful for my cult journey and this opportunity to share it with you. Don't get me wrong, it's not one I would have purposefully chosen had I been able to see the wolf from the start. But eventually, I found my inner light at the end of the tunnel, illuminating the lessons to be learned and leading me to liberation from the clutches of a powerful cult. Should you be similarly entangled, you will find your liberation, too.

SPIRITUAL EGO

In spiritual organizations, beware of hierarchy and leaders claiming superiority.

While a strong leader can be advantageous in keeping an organization running smoothly, leading through inclusivity and empowerment versus controlling through superiority and disempowerment are two very different leadership styles. One is respected and loved; the other is isolated and feared. Superiority is the offshoot of egoic pride and narcissism, often a defense mechanism to feelings of inferiority. So, it's not surprising that someone mired in deceit and greed leads with the air of superiority.

Ego is a useful tool for engaging with the physical realm. We utilize the ego to drive us to fulfill our purpose. The ego keeps us connected to our human experience and enables us to relate to the collective. However, when the ego is the maestro of our life, we can fall into greed, corruption, and competition. The ego is looking out for number one, and when it is at the helm, it can blind us to our interconnectedness with everything around us. Its focus on personal gain and survival can be at the expense of unity, understanding, and our higher purpose. Fear-based decisions and division can result from the ego's desire for superiority and validation.

As our level of consciousness rises, we merge more and more with our inner nonphysical aspects, and the outer-focused ego can take more of a backseat. The egoic consciousness becomes quieter as we engage more from the soul level. However, we can be fooled into thinking we have tamed the ego, only to find we have developed a spiritual ego. We may feel set apart from others when we intellectually understand many advanced spiritual concepts and have possibly had some extraordinary spiritual experiences. The spiritual ego can slip in and secretly make us feel superior to others. Spiritual ego can be tricky because it is related to the soul and not our human aspect. If left unchecked, the spiritual ego can become just as toxic as the psychological ego, with a focus on making material gains at any cost.

Hierarchy, inner circles, and putting people on pedestals are likely indicators of overactive egos, including narcissism, which are the antithesis of true enlightenment. While it is so that our level of consciousness creates our reality, and as we raise our consciousness, we will generally have higher experiences, attaining and sustaining higher states of consciousness is not the job of the ego. Rather, we experience the higher levels of consciousness through our soul. Releasing the ego is necessary to open more to higher awareness.

Things get convoluted when spiritual heights are attained, and then the ego steps in to claim them. When the ego is driving, the unique and mystical experiences that can accompany peak spiritual events lead to a feeling of being special or chosen when, in fact, raising our consciousness and experiencing the Divine is a potential within everyone.

Being aware of the risk of developing a spiritual ego helps to navigate the cult potential as you engage with spiritual teachers. Condescension, airs of superiority, neediness for validation, and continuous emphasis on their proclaimed spiritual or psychic gifts and talents are potential indicators of a spiritual ego at play and a ripe setting for a cult.

CULT MENTALITY IN NON-SPIRITUAL ORGANIZATIONS

The cult experience extends beyond spiritual teachers. The same dynamic can be found in yoga studios, personal development programs, coaching programs, alternative health companies, multi-level marketing, start-ups, and more traditional religions.

I had a fascinating conversation about this with Scott Homan on my podcast.[24] Scott made a film about escaping a religious cult. I was aware of the religion in question but never thought of it as a cult before meeting Scott.

He was very clear that growing up in his religion's culture was very much a cult experience. When he started to wake up to the mind control happening within his local group and began extracting himself from it, he noticed the same cult-mentality in other areas of life, including work environments centered around a charismatic founder or CEO. I have also seen people idolize their career coaches in a guru-type fashion, with the coaches lapping it up and strengthening their egos through the admiration.

I know of people who have joined various business coaching programs only to find the charismatic leader of the program is essentially training them on methods for manipulating their clients into becoming dependent on them, agitating prospective clients' problems to create the illusion of need served only by the services offered, or other creative ways of preying upon clients to gain money and control. If it weren't true, it would be laughable that the predatory behavior these coaching programs teach is the same one used to lure their clients. So, the cycle of depravity continues, as does the hook and lure of the cult culture.

Be aware of this human tendency to idolize others and hand over power to those with more experience. It's about finding balance, keeping what is beneficial, and letting the rest go. Mentors, teachers, and guides serve a purpose and can help us accelerate our learning and development. But it is important to stay true to ourselves and not blindly follow anyone. Humans have a very hard time keeping power from getting the best of them, and the more of our power we give to another, the more likely their demands for our power will intensify to our detriment. When we prioritize our sovereignty and keep our connection to our Higher Self strong, we can navigate any treacherous detours we may find ourselves on and come out with more wisdom, clarity, and a new resolve. We become rooted in truth with guidance from our Higher Self and divine team. We alchemize challenges into growth and emerge more aligned with our inner purpose.

_do it!_

If you are involved in any spiritual or religious organization or personal development program, I invite you to bravely and honestly assess whether your participation is really serving *your* own highest good or *theirs*—the charismatic leader or organization.

Reading my cult story, perhaps you were thinking, "My goodness, Kara, where was your head? I mean, all those warning signs you had even before you took a deep dive. How could you not see this was a cult?"

I know. I KNOW. It all seems incredibly obvious now. Even then, as I was wading deeper into the cult, I had my suspicions and kept looking around, wondering if things were not as they appeared. But the gravitational pull of the whole experience kept me tethered until my eyes were opened and shifted my center of gravity back to me and my own divinity, and I broke free. Still, it was very hard to face the realization that I'd given my time, attention, love, and money to a cult.

Seeing something I had trusted and believed in as concealing a cesspool of control and manipulation required an inner paradigm shift and a healthy dose of bravery and humility.

If you are ready to take an inner journey to test your own vulnerability, here are some questions and behaviors to explore that may help determine if you are unwittingly involved in a cult or cult-like organization.

- Are you being manipulated and siphoned for your money, time, energy, connections, body, or adoration?

- Are you willingly inserting a seemingly infallible authority between you and God? Are you deferring to someone else, believing they truly hold the key to your enlightenment?

If thinking about any of that gives you a sensation of suspicion or concern, I invite you to go deeper and review this list of common tactics used by cult leaders and be honest about whether any apply to your situation, indicating a possible cult organization:

- Members give extraordinary amounts of money relative to their means to support the core cause.

- Members are openly encouraged to evangelize for the purpose of recruiting new followers and money.

- Members are encouraged to sever ties with family and friends.

- The group leader is a self-fashioned guru who claims to be the sole liaison between you and God.

- Teachings are presented as the one true or quickest path to enlightenment.

- Members are warned not to read or engage with other spiritual or religious teachings as this will poison their path to enlightenment.

- There are allegations or proof of sexual misconduct within the organization.

- The organization and leader have complete dominance over your life both inside and outside the organization.

If you recognize any of these tactics at play in your life, I hope my story and the stories of countless others you can find will stand as encouragement and inspiration to be honest with yourself about your situation and get out of this toxic environment.

Truly, bravely own the part you played so you can learn from it. Temper that with compassion and forgiveness of yourself, and even allow some congratulations for going through it and being ready to come out the other side. It's no small test! In many ways, it is a type of initiation many people go through.

If you have made it this far in this book, you are clearly committed to your spiritual growth. Liberation is a requirement of mastery. Free yourself. Trust when it's time to release the lesson, forgive, and move on.

CHAPTER 10

TIME OUTSIDE OF TIME

My spiritual journey has sometimes been a magical Disney ride and, at other times, more like a weird and unexpected Meow Wolf moment. Both have brought me deeply profound and wonderous spiritual gifts and growth, but in unique and wildly different ways—one easy, familiar, predictable, and the other unexpected, untamed, and unforeseen.

The more familiar Disney aspects of my spiritual journey have included a deep sense of calm as my default operating mode. This inner peace allows me to consistently hold a spiritual perspective when facing life's challenges rather than dropping into worry about the unending threat of possible undesirable outcomes. The magic of this centeredness has also given me a heightened intuition, empowering me to be at the right place and connect with the right people at the right time more often.

The strange and unexpected aspect of my spiritual journey is not as easily explained or understood, but Meow Wolf is a great analogy. Meow Wolf is an immersive, interactive art installation with secret passages, surreal environments, and otherworldly realms that vividly stimulate multiple senses simultaneously, leaving you in a state of sheer wonderment that is difficult to recall and describe later. Meow Wolf installations are analogous to the multidimensional dream state experiences I described earlier in this book.

Like the interactive exhibits, my nighttime adventures simultaneously stimulate multiple senses on the inner planes of psychic seeing, hearing, feeling, and knowing. With so much happening at once in this inner world, sensory overload keeps me from remembering more than just a small fraction of the experience, and my little Kara self can't grasp a meaningful way to understand or describe the totality of the experience. Like Meow Wolf, it's an inexplicably strange and exhilarating experience, but there's nothing like *weird* to captivate my curiosity for diving beneath the surface. Of the many unusual concepts I have chased down the proverbial rabbit hole, time is one of the weirdest.

Time is Weird

When my multidimensional, inner Meow Wolf experiences began, I was familiar with the concept that time is an illusion and that at a quantum level, everything is happening in an eternal now. I had accepted such concepts theoretically, but it was difficult for my rational mind to truly understand them.

A hallmark of mystical experiences is that what felt like hours on the inner plane is only minutes in real-time, and vice versa, what felt like minutes is hours on a clock. It is also common for people who have a near-death experience, also called an NDE, to be clinically dead for only minutes but have far-reaching, long out-of-body experiences, which can include engaging with loved ones who have passed, having a life review with a guide, flying throughout the Universe, and many more experiences that would take much longer in Earth time. Apart from mind-bending time lapses, there's the question of whether linear time even exists beyond a mental construct for navigating the material world. Many esoteric wisdom teachings are rooted in the view that there are actually no *past* and *future* lives, only multiple lives happening simultaneously in an eternal now present.

Ok, but I experience time all the, well, *time*. It is part of my daily life. So, how can it be just an illusion?

Time as a Spiral

Fortunately, my nighttime mystical experiences provided some answers to the question of the *time being an illusion* mystery. As I explained earlier, during my first ethereal venture, I passed through numerous realms, witnessing them for a while before being lifted to the next one. I saw some realms as colors that dissolved to expose another realm behind them that consisted primarily of geometrical forms. Beyond that, I rose further into space, where I looked out of two octagonal or hexagonal windows framed in metal with tiny symbols. Next, I saw a multitude of very thin golden lines intersecting in what seemed to be infinite ways, which I understood to be a kind of code system administered by unseen beings.

Next, I was looking down upon a complex spiral, similar to a circular labyrinth. I understood this to represent *time*. From this perspective, I understood that every moment was represented in this spiral, and wherever I placed my attention within the spiral would take me to a specific moment in time. My strange, mystical experience at that precise moment was a point in this magical time spiral. I remember feeling that I was having a temporal experience while simultaneously *witnessing myself* in that time-space experience. I told you— totally Meow Wolf stuff!

Focusing on the labyrinth of time, I noticed depth and levels connected to each time-space experience in the spiral, which seemed related to the concept of timelines. Each experience had a vibrational range, allowing for various timelines to unfold depending on the vibrational match of the experiencer. In other words, focusing my attention on one point within the time spiral could result in a lower or higher vibrational experience—or anywhere in between— depending on my intention and level of consciousness. Being open and accepting or closed off and suspicious creates different vibrational levels of my experience.

Imagine I'm at a workshop, learning something new. I can be curious, willing, excited, and supportive of fellow participants and the instructor, setting myself up for a higher vibrational experience. Or I could be suspicious, doubtful, impatient, and generally negative, setting me up for a lower vibrational experience. Bringing a higher vibrational frequency to the experience triggers a more optimal timeline to unfold in the spiraling sequence for that event. The sequence I have set in motion also interacts with the group, lifting the collective experience and sending back a higher frequency experience to me. The same is true if I input a lower vibrational frequency, which sets me up for a less-than-optimal experience. My vibrational match draws the lower-level experience to me and makes the higher experience less accessible. Literally, what goes into the spiral comes out of the spiral!

Another way of describing the spiral of time experience is by analogy to dropping a turntable needle on a spinning vinyl record. Whatever groove the needle lands in determines the music played. Similarly, wherever the needle lands in the time spiral determines what is experienced. The difference is that while a vinyl record is flat with only one version of the song that can be played, the time spiral has innumerable layers and depths to what can be played. Emanating a higher vibration when dropping the needle on the spot in the time spiral results in it playing a vibrational match experience. A lower vibration instructs the needle to *play* a lower experience.

Back to my metaphysical experience, as I absorbed the profundity of time as a multi-leveled, interactive spiral, I wondered what would happen if I shifted my focus and *brought the needle down* on another part of the spiral. So, I jumped my focus to the left and immediately saw an image of a girl who was about nine or ten years old. Above her was a big, cloudy sky. She was standing by a horse in front of a tall, narrow stone house with a big tree nearby. I understood it was around the 1800s and seemed to be in Britain, possibly Scotland.

The little girl didn't look like me, necessarily, and I didn't have a clear indication of whether this was me in a past life or if it was simply an example of how this was also an event happening *now* from the perspective of the spiral rather than that of linear time. I didn't stay with the vision of the girl and the horse long enough to gain insights into their meaning beyond the idea that this part of the time spiral contained another person in another time and place from my own. On reflection, it seems logical that this would either be a past or a parallel life of mine. But truthfully, that is conjecture or interpretation rather than definitive knowledge acquired through the experience.

I was fascinated by the vivid imagery of my time spiral experiences, and for a while, I thought this was just how time *worked*. I've since been surprised to see time illustrated in other ways in other mystical journeys. Leave it to the Universe to not be boxed in!

The Space-Time Continuum

In another time outside of time experience on the inner planes, I was adrift in space, a dark void with no floor, ceiling, or walls. Gradually, I began to see enormous round shapes appear. They were made of very thin, silvery circular lines. As they came more into focus, they appeared as huge rotating gears oriented vertically. Next, I noticed what looked like a galaxy rotating horizontally, similar to a vision that appeared to me in my first few months of developing a meditation practice, which left me completely confused at the time but has become a very familiar and rather common visual to appear in my mind's eye.

Combined, the rotating gears appeared as one plane and the rotating galaxy as another. I related the vertical orientation of the gears to time, as represented by the *y-axis* on a coordinate plane graph, and the horizontal orientation of the galaxy to space, as represented by the *x-axis*. The intersection point of the two axes is the time-space coordinate where we experience physical reality. As we go through life, we are moving along an energy grid that inherently converges at space-time coordinates or x and y-axis intersection points. These planes of space and time overlap and thus intersect each other, and the angle at which they intersect determines the timeline and frequency level of the lived experience at that moment.

While the mechanism of these time-space intersecting axes seemed very logical and coherent in my heightened metaphysical state, I don't have all of the appropriate language to convey it completely. There were elements of the intersection's angle of the time and space planes that related to the vibrational frequency of the person having the experience, which, in turn, determined their perception or level of experience. It was like the angle of the intersection of the axes bent the light in a certain way relative to the vibrational frequency of the one having the experience, dictating how they felt about the experience. Though the apparatus of intersecting axes was a different depiction of how time and space converge, it was similar to the concept of a record needle being dropped on a groove in the time spiral.

To think of how this works practically in your own life, consider the date, time, and location of your life experiences correlating to convergence points where your x and y-axis intersect. Every moment of your life has occurred at some point in time, moving you along the y-axis of time. You were born, took your first step, went to kindergarten, turned sixteen, and had your first day of work on different dates in linear time. All those same life events happened at different locations, moving you along the x-axis of space. Every other moment of your life has occurred at a precise time and location of an x and y-axis intersection.

As you move through these x and y-axis intersections, you have thoughts, feelings, and perspectives related to what is occurring at that time-space moment. These thoughts, emotions, and mental constructs interact with the space-time convergence, projecting light into the void and creating your experience of reality. I understood the concept is analogous to how a movie projector works to illuminate an image on a screen. Applied to my x and y-axis experience, our eyes are the projector. Light is projected *through* the eyes at the x and y-axis convergence point, illuminating a holographic image that we experience as reality.

What struck me most about this vision was the idea that the external experience was *being created through the observation* of the one in the experience. There was no creation outside what the person was seeing through their projecting of physical reality. They were creating their reality through their own eyes as they moved along through space-time.

Back to Reality

As fascinated as I was by my experiences of time from such quantum perspectives, it could be tempting to accept these insights as merely theoretical mind-play without any practical application to everyday life. But here on Earth, time and space are very much a part of our lived experience. Gaining an understanding of these concepts at a deeper universal and energetic level, beyond how we measure them with clocks and maps, can significantly impact how we experience life as we know it.

Although the time-space continuum establishes the temporal and spatial boundaries of reality, the light of our consciousness projected through our human lens creates our experience of it, opening up immeasurable possibilities about how we create our reality and engage with the quantum field. With just this level of understanding, we can see how it's possible for consciousness to project through time-space from one x and y-axis intersection to another.

One area where we see the immediate effects of working outside the traditional concept of time and space is energy healing, which has been around for millennia, well before the age of modern medicine. It is not even necessary for a skilled energy healer to be physically present with the person receiving their healing energy for the healing to be effective and profound.

Understanding that time and space are illusionary also helps explain how prayer works to transform reality from distant shores around the world.

It is helpful to keep in mind that we do not need to *send* prayers in the same way we exert force to move things physically from one place to another. Unlike physical objects, the energy of prayers is a vibrational force that moves through the ethers. Prayers work remotely to effect change for the recipient at the right x and y-axis intersection point. Unlike throwing a ball, exerting force to throw a prayer as far as possible doesn't work. For example, if we are in the US and praying for a friend in Asia, we might think that in order for our prayers to reach them, we have to exert some kind of force for the energy of our prayer to reach them in Asia. But by applying force, we are unintentionally contracting our energy, which is counterproductive to cultivating healing energy. It is far more efficient to be relaxed in our focus as we pray or bring energetic healing to another. This allows our energy to grow and expand to facilitate positive change. In that expanded state, we are routing our prayers through the backend grid system to easily access any x and y-axis intersection point of consciousness beyond time and space limitations.

Timeline Escapades

The knowledge I gained through my Meow Wolf adventures in time shaped my understanding of timelines. The concept of timelines comes up quite a bit in metaphysical circles. As one might think, a timeline is essentially a sequentially occurring series of events—a *this then that* linear progression. Considering this from the perspective of the time-space continuum, this would be the sequential progression from one x and y-axis intersection to the next.

But what if there are multiple planes of reality— multidimensional realms where we exist simultaneously in different time-space realities? What if each of those realities represents a separate timeline trajectory? What if each projection of consciousness onto the x and y-axis intersection affects multiple timelines?

These are all big questions that have been addressed by an increasingly commonly held view that multiple timelines—perhaps infinite—are running simultaneously in the multiverse of our lives at an individual and collective level. These timelines may be viewed as stacked or intersecting in the time spiral, but each has its own trajectory in the time-space continuum. Under this view, every decision point creates multiple timeline possibilities depending on the next choice point, and each choice gets played out in its own timeline, giving infinite, very real meaning.

This concept can easily tire out the rational brain as we try to think of these infinite versions of ourselves and all the possibilities of choices that are playing out. Pay attention to the little choices you have in just one hour, and imagine how many parallel timelines would be created from each choice point:

- You sleep in, or you get up.

- You meditate, or you go for a walk.

- You have breakfast or don't have breakfast.

- You do have breakfast, but you go out for breakfast, or you eat at home.

- You ask a friend to meet you for breakfast, or you dine alone.

These are just a few examples of routine decisions we don't even need to put much thought into, but each of those choices builds up to create a unique day for us, which is a different day than if we make a different choice at any point. Our choices build upon each other, and new choices can present based on our previous choices, which wouldn't present based on a different choice.

For instance, if you choose to go out to breakfast rather than stay home, you may have a chance encounter with someone you wouldn't have met otherwise. That person may have a problem weighing them down, for which you happen to have the skill set to solve. This can lead to a job opportunity that falls into your lap unexpectedly. Had you slept in or stayed home, your day and potentially even your life could have been very different than what transpired from the choice to have breakfast out. This chance encounter creates a completely different timeline possibility for you than if you had stayed home.

Of course, we have to make much bigger choices than where to eat breakfast. We have to make patently life-changing decisions about education, work, partners, children, finances, and health that significantly impact the timeline we know and live out. The college we choose determines what courses of study we can pursue and what employment opportunities we can have. When we graduate, the company we work for will likely impact where we live, which influences who we will meet based on locale.

Changing any of these big choices alters the possible timeline trajectories, dramatically shifting what life would look like years down the road. According to the multiple timelines theory, not only are these other timeline trajectories possible, but they actually happen in alternate realities in which other versions of ourselves are living out the timelines of the other choices we could have made.

There is a movie with Gwyneth Paltrow called *Sliding Doors* that beautifully illustrates the concept of timelines.[25] The film is centered upon a pivotal moment when the main character either catches or misses her subway train. From that one event, the movie splits into two narratives and follows the unfolding of her life based on whether she caught her train or not. In one timeline, making the earlier train means she arrives home early and catches her partner cheating on her, causing her to leave him and make a fresh start. In the other timeline, she misses the train, doesn't discover her partner's infidelity, and carries on her life with him. As the film builds, it illustrates how seemingly small choices or events can culminate in wildly different outcomes in relationships, careers, personal growth, and even hairstyles.

Thinking of this brought to mind my own experience with traversing the possibility of multiple timelines.

Should I Stay or Should I Go Now?

In my twenties, I moved to England to be near the guy I was dating, who is now my husband. We dated long-distance for a while, but eventually, it was time to try living on the same continent. So, I moved to England with our long-term plan to make our home in the US. We married a couple of years later and were happy in England. I loved the country and culture. We had great friends and loved the ease with which we could travel to diverse places to experience new countries and cultures.

We always wanted to have a family, and the time to have a baby drew closer and closer. As two years of living in England turned into three, and babies started to come into focus for us and our friends, the decision loomed about whether we would indeed move to the States as originally planned or start a family in England and settle down there.

There were an overwhelming number of factors to consider, and the decision to relocate was extremely difficult. There were powerful pluses and minuses on each side of the stay-or-go equation. I diligently thought through each possibility and would think I'd come to a decision, only to rethink it all again and become equally convinced about the opposite choice. I made spreadsheets and tried to give different weights to each pro and con, struggling to quantify the value of various aspects of life, such as length of maternity leave, cost of living, and job opportunities.

After four years in England, we decided to go. We moved back to the US, but I never was 100% convinced it was the right choice. While I was happy enjoying the everyday conveniences of life in the US and having my family around, I missed our friends and my husband's family on the other side of the pond. I was sorry that our two kids wouldn't get to spend much time with their grandparents and cousins there. Their childhood, education, and even their accents would have been so different if we had stayed. I have said many times since we made that decision to move to the US that I really wish I could have a parallel life where we stayed in England with the kids and could experience both options simultaneously instead of having one life at the cost of the other.

The concept of timelines lies directly in that sentiment of desiring parallel experiences of staying or going. It expands out as we break it down to all the other choices that stem from those choices and how everyone we are connected with is also making their choices, and our choices intersect or not based on what we choose. It's a lot for the rational mind to try to wrap itself around!

Playing the Record of Our Timeline

I have wondered if the multiple timeline theory might explain the depth and layering I saw in my time spiral experience. Going back to the analogy of the record needle being dropped on a point in the spiral and playing out a vibrationally higher or lower experience of that moment, depending on the depth of the layer it follows, I see a correlation between those layers and timelines. Dramatically simplified, the layers on the time spiral would relate to how each point, as a moment or event, can be experienced at a higher or lower frequency— joyful, neutral, or negative, with each experience playing out as a different timeline with a different outcome. In other words, the layers are timelines diverging from a single moment in time.

Conversely, we can also think of timelines as predicting the events we will experience. Although this view suggests that we are at the mercy of these events, it's just a different way of understanding that while we may not control what happens—where the needle lands—we absolutely can decide how we respond to it—the layer we choose to play. We are innately empowered with the ability to choose our response, creating our individualized experience of reality. The more we understand that our choices create our experience, the more we can take responsibility for our own happiness. Our joy comes more and more from our inner world and less from what is happening in the outer world as we learn to shift our focus from the event to our empowered choices in responding to it.

The concept of timelines helps us understand that there are no set outcomes for anything we experience. Our choices are influenced by the timeline we are on, and we influence the timeline we are on by our choices. We are continuously influencing the level of our experience through our vibration, responses, and intentions. The more we can embody the understanding of timelines and the ways we unconsciously choose the one we are experiencing, the more we can keep that record needle playing the high-frequency experiences.

Let's have a bit of fun with what we have learned about timelines. According to this quantum concept of timelines, there are innumerable versions of you in the quantum sense.

Consider that there is a version of you, in my reality, who understands that there are innumerable versions of you from a quantum perspective. Another version of you in your reality thinks this is all just mind-bendy babble that makes no sense and that your current experience is the only possibility. This version of you is curious but did not drop the needle on a choice point of diving into the quantum theory of multiple timelines.

Both versions are perfect for each timeline, respectively. What is so fun is that because the version of you in my reality *does* understand timeline possibilities, it's a part of you that is accessible in the quantum. In that timeline, we laugh and celebrate the fact that both versions of you, the one who understands timelines and the one who doesn't, are the same person—just a slight needle drop away in the time spiral. Adjacent to that groove in the time spiral is another potential with a version of you who initially doesn't understand this chapter, then comes across it again in the future, has a total timeline epiphany, and finds this all very, very funny, indeed!

do it!

It's journal time! Think of a recent event that caused some sort of response within you. Perhaps you were embarrassed, insulted, or misunderstood.

Write down what happened, your response, and how you felt.

- Next, consider where this response would fall in terms of the spectrum of possible responses, from low to high frequency.

- Did this event cause you to become angry, sad, guilty, or ashamed, which would be responses on the lower side of the spectrum? Or was your response joyful, loving, or compassionate—the higher side of the spectrum—or something in the middle?

- Make a note of where your response falls on the spectrum. Strive to maintain some neutrality within yourself as you honestly evaluate the level of your response without tipping into judgment of the other person or yourself.

- Now imagine that the record needle came down at another level of that event, and your response was different according to that level.

- What would a high level have looked like, presuming yours was not already the highest response you can think of? Are there any judgments, assumptions, or misunderstandings on your part that colored your perspective, and without them, could the record needle have been at a higher place?

AFTERWORD

The spiritual journey is never complete. It is an unending pursuit of aligning with your highest and best self as you reach each new summit. Certain peaks on your ascent will stand out as experiences of the Divine that forever shift your perception of reality. Inevitably, you must navigate the descent from such spiritual heights back into the physical world of our collective reality. But, hopefully, with each peak experience, you come back into the material world a little wiser about yourself and the nature of reality with greater compassion and appreciation for all life, including yours. After all, you chose to incarnate in a human body for a particular reason in this Earthly realm with all its unique expressions of duality to promote evolution and spiritual growth.

This physical plane and the human experience always serve to expand the soul. Your life is an amazing opportunity for your soul's development. Each obstacle you encounter reveals a chance to let go of previous patterns, limitations, and perspectives that keep you locked into a smaller version of yourself. Step by step, brick by brick, you are creating your life.

Enjoy the ride!

It can be easy to take life way too seriously. Yes, being alive is an important experience, and life is precious and sacred. We are here to live, love, grow, and learn through experience. So, why not allow that experience to be fun? You can learn with laughter and joy in your heart. Don't buy into the old paradigm of learning through suffering.

That is not to say there won't be challenging moments on your journey, but you can choose how you will learn through that experience. You can absorb the lesson, then let yourself off the hook and apply what you learned to the next opportunity for growth. You can be silly and place less value on what others think of you while remaining dedicated to being wiser, more compassionate, and understanding every day.

Your life gets to be whatever you want it to be.

Give yourself space to breathe, relax, and let go of the expectations of yourself and others. If you find yourself returning to patterns you thought you had already overcome, try again. Keep going. Dedicate yourself to expanding your consciousness through your spiritual growth and evolution. Remember that it doesn't happen all at once but gradually through every choice you make. Soul expansion happens at your pace, fueled by your desire for change and growth.

Every day, you can engage with life in ways that move you more quickly toward aligning with more awake, aware, and higher versions of yourself. At the end of each chapter, I offered some exercises to help you realize how even simple everyday choices make a big difference on your spiritual journey. Every moment of your life is an invitation to express the pure beauty of your soul's true nature and essence. Each situation presents an opportunity to let go of old, outdated patterns and choose a new response.

Never forget that your spiritual journey is unique to you.

Authentic soul growth isn't neatly packaged in some pre-formatted program created by someone else where you tick the boxes until you reach enlightenment. Learn from others who are further along the path than you but also stand confidently in your authentic self. Know that there will be methods, teachings, and modalities that your soul is attracted to but that may not be aligned for someone else. Your soul is guiding you. Listen.

Your life is happening right now, right where you are. The life you are here to live is not in some dreamed-of future or long-remembered past. It's right in front of you here and now. Take time to place yourself in the present moment. Notice when and where you are and the experience unfolding before you—then and there. Trust that, despite appearances, whatever is happening in your life now is specifically designed by you for your highest and best good, leading you to your highest potential for expanding consciousness and spiritual growth.

Opportunities for expansion are cleverly designed as challenges, frustrations, and obstacles. Without these friction points, we don't get the opportunities we need to overcome for growth. When we are comfortable, we coast. Imagine going to the gym and riding a stationary bike or lifting weights without weight resistance. While still going through the motions of exercising, there's no resistance to develop muscle strength. So it is with life. Without experiencing some resistance to knock us out of our comfort zones, we tend to go through the motions of daily living without making much progress toward building the muscles we need for awakening to the truth of who we are, expanding into ever higher versions of ourselves.

Appreciate the life you have.

It is not a mistake that you are here. Your soul wanted to come and experience the unique opportunities in living a human life. Take advantage of your physical presence in the world and recognize the spiritual importance of your human life. Western culture doesn't always make it easy to hold and nurture a spiritual perspective on life. Making your spiritual journey a priority can feel foreign, overwhelming, and confusing. The further you go down the path, the more it can feel like you are losing who you were, and, in a sense, that's true. Any period of growth demands the release of things that don't serve you on the path ahead. Surrendering to the unknown and letting go of old patterns, beliefs, people, and places that aren't aligned with your soul's journey is non-negotiable for accelerating your spiritual awakening and expansion.

Be your authentic You.

Despite the external appearance of change and uncertainty on your journey, there is an eternal and ever-present aspect of yourself buried underneath the rubbish of conditioning and habituated self-sabotage that has kept it hidden from view. This aspect of you is the truth of who you are as a Divine being, an eternal soul. Your spiritual journey is the discovery and reclamation of this part of you, your authentic self.

I sincerely hope this book has helped you acquire some valuable tools for your journey of soul discovery. You also have the help of your guides on the inner planes and in the physical world, who are ever present and ready to assist you even when you don't know how to ask for their help.

Be Brave!

The voyage is worth it. The truth of who you are is waiting for you to step forward and stand in the vast wisdom, beauty, and glory of your authentic you.

Book Club Questions

1. Reflecting on your lifestyle, in what moments or circumstances do you feel most connected to your soul and open to inspiration beyond your five traditional senses? What new practices could you incorporate to deepen and nurture that connection?

2. What resistances or challenges arise when you consider strengthening your connection to your soul and Higher Self? For example, do you face obstacles like societal expectations, a demanding schedule, fear of the unknown, or self-doubt? How might you begin to address these?

3. Have you experienced moments of expanded consciousness, where deeply held beliefs gave way to new, more expansive understandings? What led to those shifts, and how did they impact your perspective on life?

4. What external influences—such as family, media, education, and societal norms—have the strongest impact on your beliefs and decisions? How might you reclaim your power from these influences if they do not feel aligned with your soul?

5. Do you currently engage in practices such as meditation, energy work, nature, or journaling—to strengthen your energy fields and connect with your Higher Self? What practice or practices have had the most positive impact?

6. Looking ahead, what are three changes or transformations you would like to experience in the next six months? What small steps can you take today to set those changes into motion?

7. Can you identify any hidden fears that might be holding you back? Have you utilized any practices to help you release or transform those fears?

8. When you connect with the energy of your heart, what sensations or signals do you notice? These could be physical feelings, emotional shifts, or psychic impressions. How do these signals guide you in your daily life?

9. Reflect on a time when your perception of reality differed significantly from someone else's. How might stepping into their perspective help you gain a deeper understanding of their view? How might this shift in perspective impact your relationships?

10. Have you witnessed cult-like behaviors or tactics in organizations you have participated in, whether spiritual or secular? What were the most significant warning signs, and how did you navigate or remove yourself from that environment?

ENDNOTES

1. "Awake: The Life of Yogananda," directed by Paola di Florio (2014, Roco Films).

2. Stanislav Grof, *Psychology of the Future: Lessons from Modern Consciousness Research* (State University of New York Press, 2000), 136.

3. *Superhuman: The Invisible Made Visible,* directed by Caroline Cory (Omnium Media, 2020); *Among Us*, directed by Caroline Cory (Omnium Media, 2019).

4. https://news.harvard.edu/gazette/story/2011/01/eight-weeks-to-a-better-brain/.

5. Donna Eden and David Feinstein, Ph.D., *Energy Medicine: Balancing Your Bodie's Energies for Optimal Health, Joy, and Vitality* (Tarcherperigee, 2008).

6. Donna Eden Energy Medicine, "8 Energy Healing Exercises You Can Do at Home | Donna Eden's Daily Energy Routine," YouTube video, 11:48, November 5, 2022; https://www.youtube.com/watch?v=clkHOIkPaks.

7. Wim Hof, *The Wim Hof Method: Activate Your Full Human Potential* (Sounds True Adult, 2022); https://www.wimhofmethod.com/; Wim Hof YouTube Channel, https://www.youtube.com/@wimhof1.

8. https://link.springer.com/article/10.1007/s11469-020-00363-4.

9. https://soulelevationpodcast.com/jamie-butler.

10. https://www.soulelevationpodcast.com/maureen-stgermain2.

11. https://sandrawalter.com/.

12. https://booksonthewall.com/blog/leo-tolstoy-quote/#:~:text=of%20all%20time.-,Leo%20Tolstoy%20Quote,one%20thinks%20of%20changing%20himself."

13. Jill Bolte Taylor, Ph.D., *My Stroke of Insight: A Brain Scientist's Personal Journey* (Viking, 2008), 146.

14. "Finding Nemo," directed by Andrew Stanton and Lee Unkrich (2003, Los Angeles, CA; Pixar Animation Studios for Walt Disney Films).

15. Inspired by the work of Georgia Jean, Circle Evolution https://circleevolution.com.

16. https://www.heartmath.org/research/research-library/energetics/energetic-heart-bioelectromagnetic-communication-within-and-between-people/.

17. https://www.heartmath.org/research/science-of-the-heart/energetic-communication/.

18. https://www.heartmath.org/research/research-library/dissertations/correlated-heart-rate-measures-in-the-study-of-nonlocal-human-connectedness/.

19. https://www.heartmath.org/heart-coherence/.

20. Dr. David R. Hawkins, *Power vs. Force: The Hidden Determinants of Human Behavior* (Veritas Publishing, 1995).

21. Id., 52-53.

22. Neale Donald Walsch, *The God Solution* (Phoenix Books, Inc., 2020); https://www.themeditationconversation.com/185-the-god-solution-neale-donald-walsch/.

23. https://drjoedispenza.com; Richard Rudd, *The Gene Keys: Embracing Your Higher Purpose* (Watkins Publishing, 2013); https://genekeys.com.

24. https://www.soulelevationpodcast.com/Scott-Homan/.

25. "Sliding Doors," directed by Peter Howitt (1998, Miramax Films).

Acknowledgments

I extend my heartfelt gratitude to the many souls who have brought this book to life.

To my husband, children, parents, brothers, and in-laws, thank you for your steadfast love and encouragement as I have ventured onto paths less traveled. Your lightheartedness and open-mindedness as I explore the periphery of conventional understanding mean so much to me. I am deeply grateful for your support in my journey of discovery.

To Michael Massey, your spiritual guidance and mentorship over the years have been instrumental in shaping my ability to write this book. You have not only helped me navigate the often-disorienting terrain of multidimensional experiences but have also provided invaluable validation for the insights and revelations that have emerged in quantum realms. I am profoundly grateful for your wisdom, unwavering support, and, most importantly, your friendship.

To the Healing Hearth community, thank you for your boundless love and encouragement over the years. Being part of this radiant group of souls is a profound honor and joy. Our shared moments in meditation, thoughtful discussions, and book club gatherings are a true blessing, and I treasure the connections we've built together.

To my Power of 8 Group, your dedication to uplifting and supporting one another is a source of deep inspiration. It is a privilege to be part of this dedicated and transformative team. Witnessing the incredible results of our collective loving attention and focus on manifesting each member's highest intentions has been both fascinating and humbling.

To Angela (Andi) Rosenau of Sacred Dragon Publishing Services LLC, your editing wizardry has not only elevated this book but also transformed it into a tapestry more beautiful than I could have imagined. Your exceptional advice, insightful suggestions, and enthusiastic support have been invaluable throughout this journey. Working with you has been an absolute joy, and I am deeply grateful for your talent, wisdom, and guidance.

To Emily Shoop of RAY Studio, thank you for gracing this book with your stunning cover art. I am forever grateful to have your talent imprinted on this work that is so close to my heart. Our friendship of more than 25 years is one of my life's great gifts. I am honored to call such a gifted, kind, and hilariously wonderful soul my best friend.

To Lisa Sarjeant, your eagle eye and meticulous proofreading have been a tremendous asset to this manuscript. Your feedback and insights have been invaluable. Our weekly writing playdates, where much of this book was created, have been not only productive but a source of inspiration and joy. Your wit, cleverness, and boundless gifts continue to amaze me.

To Sharon Castlen, thank you for your marketing expertise. Your guidance and support have been remarkable, and I deeply appreciate the clarity and strategy you've brought to launching this book.

To Julie Murkette, your beautiful work on the interior design concept brought this book to life in beautiful ways. Thank you for your artistry and care in ensuring every detail is just right.

To Ida Jansson, your inspired design artistry in bringing this book to completion with the wonderfully designed interior layout and cover wrap. Your artistry and attention to detail shine on every page, and I am deeply grateful for your care in ensuring each element was thoughtfully crafted. Thank you very much for your dedication and commitment to making this book truly special.

About the Speaker

Kara Goodwin, a passionate advocate for personal transformation and spiritual ascension, brings years of experience and heartfelt enthusiasm to every event. As an author and speaker, she is dedicated to helping individuals connect with their Higher Selves to find profound fulfillment and a deeper sense of purpose in life.

Through her work, Kara empowers audiences to step into a greater alignment with their souls' guidance and embrace the path of awakening. Her dynamic approach combines deep wisdom, relatable insights, and actionable steps to inspire lasting change.

Speaking Topics

Kara's engaging presentations include these topics and other topics tailored to meet the specific needs of each audience.

- **Creating a fulfilling life through authentic self-expression**: Explore how embracing your unique gifts and passions can lead to a life of deeper joy and meaning.

- **Spiritual awakening and aligning with your Higher Self**: Strengthen your connection with your inner guidance and live in harmony with your true purpose.

- **The power of meditation and mindfulness in modern living**: Reduce stress and anxiety with practical techniques that bring calm, clarity, and focus to everyday and work life, helping you thrive in a fast-paced world.

- **Shadow work and overcoming limiting beliefs**: Learn how to identify and heal hidden patterns that hold you back, transforming challenges into opportunities for growth.

Groups and Audiences

Kara's approachable style allows her to connect with a wide range of audiences and meet the unique needs of each group. Here are some examples of Kara's work with professional groups and organizations.

- **Small Businesses and Corporate Teams and Departments:** Managing stress and enhancing workplace harmony through mindfulness and meditation.

- **Women's Groups:** Inspiring empowerment and connection through shared experiences and spiritual tools.

- **Churches**: Exploring spiritual themes that align with universal truths and personal growth.

- **Non-Profits**: Emphasizing personal transformation to maximize the impact on the larger mission.

- **Retreat Centers:** Guiding experiences that deepen participants' spiritual journeys and help them connect to their souls.

Kara's enthusiasm is contagious, her insights profound, and her presence magnetic. She creates a warm and inclusive environment, making her talks a catalyst for deep reflection and meaningful action. Kara weaves practical tools with higher truths to leave participants inspired, energized, and motivated to create positive change in their lives.

To book Kara for your event, visit the speaker page on her website https://www.karagoodwin.com/speaker.

About the Author

Kara Goodwin is devoted to helping others deepen their connection to spirit and elevate their consciousness. She is passionate about making spiritual practices accessible to modern lifestyles, allowing mindfulness and meditation to be seamlessly integrated into daily routines. Through her teachings, podcasts, and retreats, she inspires others to explore their true nature, awaken to higher levels of consciousness, and experience energy shifts that transcend the intellectual mind.

Her *Soul Elevation* podcast—formerly *The Meditation Conversation*—is a platform dedicated to exploring the vast realms of consciousness and spiritual transformation. Kara invites listeners on a journey into topics such as mysticism, energy healing, miracles, angels, psychic abilities, multidimensionality, quantum physics, and more, empowering them to expand their awareness and embrace their highest potential.

Kara's spiritual journey began during a challenging chapter of her life. After working in the corporate world for 15 years, she turned to meditation as a way to cope with a series of personal tragedies. Over time, her practice evolved into a powerful tool for connecting with her Higher Self and Source, allowing her to receive divine light and codes in service of ascension. Her mystical experiences have included encounters with organized light and geometries, colors, angelic realms, and expansive states of consciousness, profoundly shaping her understanding of the universe and her purpose within it.

Kara works directly with individuals and groups through mystical retreats, private healing sessions, and her online community. As a certified meditation teacher and Reiki Master, she integrates meditation, mindfulness, and energy healing into her work, helping clients transform their lives through deeper connections to themselves and their spiritual goals. Kara offers group and private meditation lessons, as well as coaching services designed to accelerate healing and personal transformation.

Kara's podcasts, teachings, and healing sessions are imbued with high-frequency energy that supports the expansion of consciousness and empowers individuals on their spiritual journey.

INVITATION TO CONNECT

Thank you for inviting this book to be a part of your sacred journey. It is truly my honor to support you in awakening your consciousness and aligning with your authentic self. If this book has touched you, I would be so grateful if you would leave a review on your favorite online book-related site. Your sharing helps others discover this work, creating a ripple effect that raises vibrational frequencies and supports collective transformation.

I warmly invite you to connect with me and explore more resources to support your journey.

- Explore my website for more information about my services, including meditation support and healing sessions
  https://www.KaraGoodwin.com

- Discover hundreds of my podcast episodes exploring ascension and awakening
  https://www.SoulElevationPodcast.com

- Say hi and find daily inspiration on Instagram
  https://www.instagram.com/kara_goodwin_meditation/

- For more uplifting content, subscribe to my YouTube channel
  https://www.youtube.com/@soulelevationpodcast

Thank you for allowing this book to be part of your sacred path. Together, we elevate consciousness as we awaken to the infinite beauty of our souls.

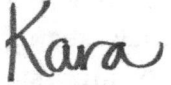

www.ingramcontent.com/pod-product-compliance
Lightning Source LLC
Chambersburg PA
CBHW060759120626
46557CB00001B/28